Luxury Selling

Francis Srun

Luxury Selling

Lessons from the World of Luxury in Selling High
Quality Goods and Services to High Value Clients

Francis Srun
Hong Kong, Hong Kong

ISBN 978-3-319-45524-2   ISBN 978-3-319-45525-9 (eBook)
DOI 10.1007/978-3-319-45525-9

Library of Congress Control Number: 2017930588

This Palgrave Macmillan imprint is published by Springer Nature
The registered company is Springer International Publishing AG
The registered company address is: Gewerbestrasse 11, 6330 Cham, Switzerland

To my wife Helen
for everything you give me
and in particular for
the idea and title of this book

Contents

About The Author

Francis Srun is a French citizen, 50 years old. He majored in Business and Administration at France's Postgraduate Business School KEDGE (Bordeaux). He also holds a Swiss Federal Professional Trainer certificate.

Srun has had a successful career in the Luxury world, being Brand Manager, International Retail Director and Managing Director with prestigious brands such as Swiss watchmaker Piaget, New York's Ralph Lauren Watch and Jewelry and French jewelry *maison* Boucheron.

Multi-cultural and with an international career, Francis Srun is fluent in French, English and Mandarin and has worked in France, Switzerland, China, Taiwan and Hong Kong.

In 2013 he published *Vendre Le Luxe* (with René Moulinier, a bestselling author) the first book ever written about selling Luxury, presenting selling techniques and customer psychology (in French).

He speaks regularly at international retail and Luxury conferences and business schools in Paris and also across Asia.

Francis Srun is the founding director of Retail Performance and can be reached at

Francis.Srun@icloud.com www.luxuryselling.com

Other Publications

Vendre Le Luxe (in French)
Techniques de vente et psychologie des clients

René Moulinier & Francis Srun, Eyrolles, 2013 Paris

Disclaimer

Please note that this book has been written by Francis Srun in a private capacity. The views expressed are his own and do not necessarily reflect those of his current or former employers.

Any resemblance to actual persons or brands is a coincidence. All examples are for illustration and educational purposes only. No brand has been directly mentioned or even suggested.

WRITTEN WITH THE VALUABLE COLLABORATION

OF

PAMELA CLOUTIER

HER EXPERTISE, PATIENCE AND "*GENTILLESSE*"

MADE THE DIFFERENCE

Pamela Cloutier, is an expert in Luxury, having held the positions of International Commercial Director, International Marketing and Trade Marketing Director and Chief Operating Officer for several prestigious timepiece and jewelry houses. With over 25 years' experience in Luxury sales and distribution strategy, Pamela consults for various Luxury brands, runs her own business in the distribution of handbags and is engaged in philanthropic and entrepreneurial projects. She has dual American and Swiss nationality and lives in Geneva, Switzerland. She may be contacted at

Pamela.G.Cloutier@gmail.com

Table Of Characters

We will tell you stories involving different sales advisors and clients. These encounters take place in Geneva, Paris, London, Hong Kong, Singapore and New York.

*** Geneva ***

Peter Wang

Peter is a very wealthy business owner, originally from Taiwan, educated in California and living between Taipei, Hong Kong, Shanghai and San Francisco. He successfully created an IT company. His passion has always being collecting timepieces. He is very knowledgeable about high-end watches and loves to spend time building his collection.

Martial Legrand

Martial is a boutique Manager for a new high-end watch brand in Geneva, Switzerland. Martial has been in the watch industry for over 15 years and would not want to move to another product category. For him, it is more than a job, it is his passion. This is especially because he has the opportunity to meet knowledgeable customers who appreciate high-end watches and with whom he is able to share the same love for these products.

*** Paris ***

Michelle and Allan Taylor

Michelle and Allan are from New York, and are visiting Paris. It is their 20th wedding anniversary trip. They are looking for some nice jewelry to celebrate this important milestone in their lives. Mr. Taylor is a reputed dentist and owns several dental care centers. Mrs. Taylor takes care of the accounting and finances of the company they founded together. They planned this beautiful, romantic trip a long time ago.

Alice Martin

Alice is a senior sales advisor at one of the most reputed high-end watch and jewelry maisons in Paris. Alice started her Luxury journey in selling fashion and a few years ago was offered the opportunity to take on her current role. She loves the new challenges—every day is a new day.

*** London ***

John Hudson

John is a Senior Vice-president, working in London for one of the top 100 UK firms. He has been recently promoted and is looking to change his current beloved family car to one of much better quality. This is an important trade-up and John wants to be sure of his choice. He did a lot of online research. He took his decision in favor of a well known German brand. He decided to visit the car showroom for a second time.

Henry Smith

Henry is an experienced sales advisor having worked for the same car brand showroom for over 15 years. He started his career selling properties. He loves cars and had the opportunity to promote them and did not hesitate for one second to change product category. Being very knowledgeable about cars, he now enjoys combining his passion for automobiles with his professional life.

*** Hong Kong ***

Lisa Lam

Lisa started her professional life as a market analyst for a top US banking firm. After her father retired, she had to take over the family interests and devoted herself to running their family office. She had to take care of the different offices in Shanghai, Hong Kong and London.

Lucy Fung

Lucy is a young sales advisor, now working for a world-class Italian leather goods brand. Lucy had tried office work but did not really like it. She loves being active and having interactions everyday with colleagues and clients. She also loves Luxury for the quality of the working environment. The daily, weekly and monthly sales pressure in the beginning was terrifying for her but now she really loves her job.

*** Singapore ***

Sophie and Thomas Williams
Sophie and Thomas are Australian citizens planning to come and live in Singapore. Thomas had the opportunity to join a Japanese firm as Chief Financial Officer but had to be based in Singapore. Sophie and the two young children are excited. Sophie has to find a new job but she is confident that she will.

Simon Cole
Simon is a property agent, specialized in premium properties. He came from London 20 years ago, preferring the sun and the humidity to the rainy UK weather. He established a small real estate agency upon his arrival, and since then has always been selling properties. He prides himself in the trust he receives from property owners and also from buyers. "The best advertising is your reputation" is his agency's tagline.

*** New York ***

Paul Morgan
Paul is in his forties and has worked for different top US firms as Marketing Manager. He was promoted to this position about 5 years ago. It has been a very busy period in his life and he really has had no time for himself or his family. He is married, with a lovely daughter and wants to take more time for his personal life, especially in planning more wisely for the twenty years ahead.

Roger Brown
Roger is a young private banking associate. He joined the century-old financial institution after graduation from one of the Ivy League universities. He learns fast and is eager to perform, to get promoted and to succeed. He is highly appreciated by his clients. In spite of his age, and with only a few years of experience, Roger has managed to quickly build a solid and long-term relationship with affluent clients.

List of Charts

List of Tables

1

Introduction

1.1 Why Did You Choose This Book?

First of all, thank you, *MERCI* for having my book in your hands.
You might have several reasons for reading *Luxury Selling*.
Your expectations might be to learn about Luxury, selling in general, customer relations management, communication and so forth. You are looking to make improvements in these areas.

You have done well. Many people want to improve their selling skills but few make the effort of even getting a resource book, let alone reading one. Congratulations for having already taken this first important step!

Mark's dream is to run the New York City marathon. Mark is brave and really worked hard in preparation. But, for the last three years, he has been telling himself: "I am not ready yet, this year." One day, though, he took a decision, just a two-click decision: he enrolled himself in the marathon online. The countdown started, and from that day on he had to train regularly and run the marathon. The real challenge was not to run the 42 kilometers, but to click the "Yes – I confirm" button.

1.2 We Are Selling Every Day

We are selling all the time. Selling means that we need someone else to "buy" our ideas or accept our proposal. In order to reach that agreement, we need to discuss things. This can take place at work with colleagues, at home with family members or with friends.

© The Author(s) 2017
F. Srun, *Luxury Selling*, DOI 10.1007/978-3-319-45525-9_1

At home, you come up with ideas, propose them, suggest various approaches and seek confirmation of them from your family or friends. These conversations are part of the transactions of daily life. Sometimes, you need to push further and go through arguments in order to reach a common understanding. Most of the time, the conversation ends with agreement and acknowledgment of that understanding. In a worst-case scenario, the conversation turns into an argument: each party sticks to their position. Do not worry, because this happens to all of us.

At work, there are discussions containing pros and cons and rational arguments, and where the parties involved have clear common objectives. This is usually called brainstorming, debating, case making or positive confrontation. It is about business, and all parties try their best to find the optimal solution for the company's project.

With retail selling, things are different. A sales advisor's objective is to sell. A customer's objective is not necessarily to buy. At least it is not always certain that a customer is seeking to purchase a specific brand or product, at a given price, here and now. Sales advisors frequently need to overcome some resistance.

1.3   Selling Is Not Always Easy

Peter Wang is a very wealthy Taiwanese businessman and a true connoisseur of fine luxury watchmaking. He is also one of the key collectors of high-end watches. In Geneva, Peter visits a new watch brand. The new brand is offering some great timepieces. Despite the quality of the craftsmanship and the complexity of the movement's mechanism, Peter is still hesitant. After all, this new brand sells timepieces for a six-digit US$ price tag. This brand has only been in existence for ten years—how can he trust it, compared to a brand with ten times more heritage? He also finds himself questioning the value. Ultimately, even if he decided to go for the "complication" (a timepiece equipped with a sophisticated movement) he likes, Peter is not sure about the size of the dial, nor the design of the hands. He just will not make a decision and the easiest thing for him is not to go for it at all.

Martial is the store manager of the boutique. He prides himself on being one of the most knowledgeable timepieces advisors and he really enjoys being specialized in such a way. He is always working on increasing his technical knowledge but also on keeping up to date with the market. "I might not be able to own beautiful art pieces but I have the chance, literally every day, to live with these incredible things." He has also learnt a lot and progressed a very long way. When he started out, he was not even sure why anyone would buy a watch at such prices when you can have the time on your mobile phone. He also knows that it is most important to understand the customers. Peter definitely could be a buyer. It is not about money—it never is when it's about Luxury and high-end items.

Will Martial be able to overcome Peter's doubts? How would you do it?

1.4   Luxury Creations Are About Exceptional Purchases

Mrs. and Mr. Taylor are in Paris with the idea of purchasing a nice piece of jewelry for themselves, to celebrate their twentieth wedding anniversary. At one of the most reputed jewelry boutiques, Michelle finds a beautiful diamond necklace. It is in their budget, the service is great and the sales advisor, Alice, explains the design perfectly. Michelle is nearly convinced but also thinks that she might be able to do better and should take more time to check other options. Maybe the diamonds are too small, even if they are of quite good quality? Her husband, Michael, is not sure if this is a good investment compared to getting a necklace with bigger stones. They just love the design but it is not an easy decision!

Alice has just come back from a week's vacation in the south of France, where she had been visiting her parents. She is fully recharged and is particularly pleased to be at the boutique and to meet such a nice couple this morning. She also knows that because this represents an exceptional purchase the couple will not want to make any mistake. It is very emotional too. Her experience has taught her that it is crucial to be able to reassure them so as to help Michelle and Michael decide. It's not only a piece of jewelry but also a celebration, full of meaning and emotion, for now and the future. This could be one of the most memorable experiences of their lives. Alice knows that she can be part of it and definitely wants to succeed.

How will Alice handle such an emotional and high-value purchase? How would you perform?

1.5   High-Value Products Imply A Real Decision Making Process

John Hudson is at the car dealership looking for a new car. This will be his dream car. He has already extensively and carefully checked information online. He went to the showroom for a second time, but not really to see the car. He just loves it—and can afford it. John is not really sure if his wife likes the car, though. They are going to have their first child soon, and he thinks that it is the right moment to change their car. But, at the same time, maybe it's not the right moment to spend even more money. That being said, John feels that he and his family deserve this beautiful car, with all the hard work and effort they put in every day. It is with many questions, not all of them related to the car as a product, that he enters the showroom for the 3rd time.

Henry notices that John is visiting for the 3rd time and that he looks determined. He knows that John might need a serious conversation today and that he could make a decision. "What is very fascinating in selling cars is that customers are always different but the same, in a certain way." Being very experienced, Henry knows that trust is key and that you need to find the right point, the trigger of the decision. Henry also needs to get more contracts signed: he is late this month in achieving his targets. Will he be able to make it up?

With other high-value products, there is a real decision making process involved, and this is somewhat similar to the case with Luxury creations. It is not only about the technical expertise of the sales advisor. It is to do with how you can influence the decision making process, to help customers clarify their mindset and lead them to making a positive decision in favor of your product.

How would you talk to John, so that this time he definitely signs the order form?

1.6   Complicated Products Entail Cautious Decision Making Processes

Paul, at 42 is more conscious than ever of the need to protect his family financially. He decides to consult his banker. There are many proposals, and one looks particularly attractive. By just saving some money today, after twenty years he would have quite a significant amount of revenue. Despite the graphics and examples, Paul still feels that something is wrong. HOW COULD THIS BE POSSIBLE? IT IS TOO GOOD TO BE TRUE! The banker seems competent but is not able to make John take the decision.

Roger does not consider himself to be a private banker but more a personal financial advisor. He is young and talks to senior executives. "They are, most of the time, very successful businessmen who have spent more time on their businesses than on themselves. My role is to assist them." Roger sells long-term commitment financial products and they are not that easy to understand. Even if his clients are always educated and smart, financial plans are somewhat difficult to grasp. Therefore, customers have fears. And fears are always the best reason for not deciding. "And that's why I love my role," said Roger.

Would you be able to find the right words to reassure Paul and, like Roger, succeed in selling him a financial plan?

1.7 Emotional Products Imply That The Decision Making Process Is Not Always Rational

Lisa is in real trouble. She feels like she needs a new handbag. She is thinking about her upcoming trip to Moscow, and has been looking at different possibilities but just cannot decide. She went to her favorite French brand and picked a model that she had spotted few months ago. Last week she happened to visit another boutique, to see a new bag. She did not know much about that Italian brand other than that it is really popular at the moment (she sees it in all the magazines). At the same time, she is telling herself that she could just go for a brand that she thinks is really "her"—and thus a safe choice. The sales advisor from the Italian brand is great, talking about all the qualities of the handbag and showing Lisa photos of many celebrities carrying that very model.

Lucy is on duty that day and is very happy to see a new customer coming in. She is enjoying herself at work—she loves meeting new people, and some of her clients are even becoming more like friends. Just by observing the new lady client, she knows that she is looking for something. But at the same time, her experience tells her to always take the necessary time to give proper service and fully assist a client. "A buying decision is more emotional than rational a lot of the time, and that is why it is so complicated and so fun," Lucy explains. This is also why Lucy enjoys helping her customers in "making up their minds." We will see that Lisa cannot really make up her mind.

How would you influence someone when there is a question of taste and colors?

1.8   Selling Is Great!

Since making decisions is not always easy, customers need help. The role of the sales advisor is not only to take the check at the end of the transaction.

Selling is also concerned with helping customers overcome their doubts and to achieve objectives that sometimes they do not know they even have, or at least are not very clear about. As a customer, you will certainly remember the joy when you finally decided to make a purchase after a long hesitation. It is a relief because you know you took the right decision and you were assisted in the process.

For Sophie and Thomas Williams, moving from Sydney to Singapore is a pretty big deal. They need to solve the housing issue. Thomas requires the help of a property advisor to be able to quickly find and decide on the house they want to buy. Not only is this important financially—it has to be a successful operation to ensure that all family members are well installed. It's more than selling: there is true responsibility in advising correctly and helping the lovely Williams family to achieve this important goal in their lives.

Few decisions could have been taken without the assistance of the sales advisor. Sales advisors have to be particularly competent in order to help customers through the long, complicated and emotional decision making process. This competence implies having knowledge, but also practical know-how and awareness about what is the right sort of behavior.

We aim to show you how to succeed with an innovative approach in selling to consumers. The road map for Luxury Selling will be:

1st step—To help you to be the right person, by adopting a Luxury Attitude. You are the artist and the one who can influence the situation.

2nd step—To contribute to your knowledge of luxury and high-spending clients. Your success will come from your full understanding of their mentality.

3rd step—To explain to you these customers' decision making processes. You will know how such customers behave and therefore will be able to influence them more easily.

4th step—To give you a complete method, leading to selling success in seven steps.

You will then become an active selling advisor, having the situation under control in order to achieve the best outcome.

You will find Mark, Peter, Alice and her husband, Paul, John and Lisa reappearing throughout this book. I hope the many stories will inspire you on this journey.

You can take the decision to stop reading or keep going. It is your choice.
If you do not want to keep reading this book, though, what will you do instead?
Will you achieve a better outcome for yourself, or for your work, with what you plan to do otherwise?

I hope you take this journey with *Luxury Selling* and thank you for your commitment.

Let us start!

First, we will see how to Be Luxury.

2

Be Luxury

2.1 Luxury Look

Your appearance is the first message you give a visitor. As the French say *"la première impression est souvent la bonne"* (meaning: the first impression is often the right one). It is crucial to be perceived positively, and to avoid a bad image, from which it will be nearly impossible to recover. You need to make a good first impression.

But only looking good is not sufficient. You are not only selling good products but outstanding creations and high value items. Clients are expecting the best from you and your brand. You want to build exceptional relations with customers, as they are expecting a really good experience.

Looking Luxury means that you are able to carry the brand's image—heritage, tradition, seriousness, creativity, *savoir-faire*—and be seen as an ambassador. Sales advisors have to look like they fit the brand or institution they represent.

2.1.1 Be Clean And Neat

Let us start with your body: it has to be clean from head to toe.

It might sound like unnecessary advice, but the first rule of looking Luxury is to be perfectly clean and groomed. This starts with true discipline. Look in

© The Author(s) 2017
F. Srun, *Luxury Selling*, DOI 10.1007/978-3-319-45525-9_2

the mirror before going into the boutique, check your appearance before meeting a client and practice mutual constant monitoring with members of the boutique team.

Story Corner

At one of the leading hotels in the world, the director proudly told me that he had created luxurious shower rooms for front office staff to enjoy before working. Some live far away, he explained. They often arrive with all the stress of public transportation. By inviting everyone to take a shower, enjoy a moment of peace and take time to pay attention to their appearance, staff present themselves very differently he said. They feel clean, relaxed and are much more self-confident and pleasant.

Most women know perfectly well how to take care of their hair. However, I do see many surprises with men. Although I cannot recommend only one hair style, I will suggest adopting a "consensual" style in harmony with your personality. For men, short hair is more reassuring than long (always more difficult to maintain) and it is easier to keep it looking clean and neat. Having a mustache and/or beard is challenging and should only be worn by those able to groom them every day. For ladies, hair color should preferably stay natural-looking, avoiding excessive creativity in color. Another simple piece of advice: visit a hair salon frequently because there is no better way to look perfect every day.

Nails are very often problematic. For men, just be sure to take care every week at least. Men do not want to leave nails too long but should not have them too short either. Longer nails for women give a nice feminine touch; going regularly for a manicure is a very good decision, to make sure nails are perfectly treated.

Manager's Corner

If you have the chance to visit Ralph Lauren headquarters, Madison Avenue, New York, you will be able to see a hair salon barber shop within the offices. All employees have access to Mr. Lauren's personal hairdresser. Managers have not only to be demanding, but provide the necessary means and resources to their team for achieving a successful personal Luxury Image.

Most women know perfectly well how to look good and apply the right amount and style of make-up. Selling luxury creations and high value products does not mean that you need to stand out with extraordinary make-up. For daily wear, it is about being subtle. The right taste, the finesse of the light touch will make all the difference. As the French say, "*le trop est toujours l'ennemi du bien*" (meaning: too much is always the enemy of just the right amount). You need to look natural, as if you had always has been this way.

2.1.2 Be Perfectly Dressed

Let us start with suits: a risk-free option for women and a must for men. A suit does not mean uniform and, to the contrary, a good suit should never look like a uniform. When possible (it can be always, if you make the effort to find tailoring at reasonable prices) your suit should be custom-tailored but if it cannot be, then your suit must be perfectly adjusted. Gentlemen, you also need to suffer to look good! A good suit has to fit like a glove, not like a sack. And there are so many subtleties to fitting a suit correctly.

Look at a suit as you would look at yourself. It has to express your personality and contribute to your self-branding. Pick lapels for differentiation; yes, but which size of lapel? How many buttons? Three buttons (looking serious), two buttons (looking classic) and why not a single-button suit (looking young)? There is an infinite choice of fabrics (plain, stripes) and textures and we recommend that you select something classic, with natural elegance.

> **Golden Rule Corner**
>
> You are what you look like. It is up to you to appear as who you want to be. It is about self-branding.

Women who choose to wear a suit do not need to look like "an office lady." Again, it is all about the choice of the silhouette. A suit can be very feminine, just as it can be very masculine, depending on how, and if, it is styled.

Many clients will immediately recognize the signs of fine tailoring, adopted by the sales advisor, such as working buttons on sleeves, a specific ticket pocket and the quality of the buttons used (horn).

When selecting your shirt or "*chemisier*," the safe choice is simple white or a light color which matches the suit. Again, it is all about the details: the color, the right cut for men and the appropriate feminine touch for ladies. You can play with variations in texture rather than trying to stand out with audacious bright colors.

Shoes are important to "finish" the total look. High heels contribute significantly to the feminine silhouette. One's choice of footwear is a clear sign of self-confidence for ladies and education for gentlemen. I encourage advisors to seriously invest in the very best shoes they can afford. They will be long-lasting, more comfortable and look good. Learn how to shine them perfectly! Again, a demanding customer will immediately recognize a properly done shoe shine as a sign of respect for others and of a superior education.

As you can see, we are more focused on the details in putting together what you wear than in simply creating an effect with an outstanding, colorful outfit.

2.1.3   Be Sophisticated, Simply

Sophistication will come from how you accessorize. Women need to wear some simple jewelry: earrings, necklace and rings are acceptable. Hair can be accessorized but hats are better kept for parties. Particular and careful attention needs to be paid to ladies' hosiery, which can never have a run or ladder in it. A piece of practical advice: always keep several replacement pairs of hosiery available at work in case you discover a ladder and need to make a quick change.

For men, a pocket square and tie are compulsory, in harmony. It is quite easy really: a white shirt goes with a white linen pocket square so you just have to learn on how to fold a pocket square and select a nice tie.

The next most important aspect of harmony has to be between socks and shoes. It is always about the attention you place in the smallest details, never about how much money you are spending to dress appropriately.

> *Golden Rule Corner*
> **You never stand out by only looking good, but by being yourself: elegant, gracious, charming, professional.**

For men, accessories are an expression of the creativity, humor, education and I would even say one's positive attitude toward life. About watches: preferably go for mechanical watches for men and of course avoid fancy timepieces. For women, not wearing a watch might sometimes be more appropriate as it will leave a clear wrist to model some types of jewelry, unless of course you are advising for a watch brand.

Do not forget about the other business accessories that customers will see: Pen, calculators, all types of "holders": cards, key, glasses, mobile telephone, tablet, and so on.

"Elegance consists in not being noticed" is a famous quote from George Bryan Brummell. I would add that you should not be noticed but remain remarkable. Your elegance is made of details that impress: all details need to be right, just right.

You need to work on your image as carefully as the image developed for the products you are selling. Your effort will often be recognized immediately, even rewarded by nice compliments from your clients. It has to remain simple, but with necessary sophistication.

2.1.4 Smelling Nice

It is a real art to choose a fragrance from among the huge variety on offer. I simply recommend being more "subtle" than choosing a too striking one. Be sure to wear some fragrance, but never too much. It is better to wear little and refresh it after lunch, for example. Men of course shall also wear cologne, discreetly.

Welcome to the luxury world—you are now one of the members by Looking Luxury!

> Golden Rule Corner
>
> Being Luxury is about finding the right self, a subtle person.
> Look at yourself in the mirror every day.
> Are you the one you want to be?

2.2   Luxury Speaking

As we saw in the previous section, here you became Luxury, a high-value product, through the sophisticated image you want to project. It should be the same with the words you are using, and in the way you communicate.

2.2.1 The Gentle Tone Mode

From normal communication, you are no doubt very familiar with the importance of tone. The same sentence "I love you" said in different tones can infer anything from true love to detestation. In sales, your tone must be kept gentle at all times.

Selling Luxury creations and high value products, you need first of all to reassure. You need to turn your tone to the gentle mode. It means a smiling tone—customers need to feel your smile in your voice.

Gentle also means simple: you will have to speak slowly and clearly. Probably many of your clients are not native English speakers. Even if they speak English, it does not mean that they are able to understand, especially if the rate of your speech used is too quick or unclear. Also, because your customer speaks English it does not mean that he is able to fully understand you.

You probably also know the importance of speaking at the same level as your interlocutor: do not use complicated words, avoid mysterious abbreviations and foreign words in general. It is not necessary to show your expertise by scaring or confusing your client. Your communication is simple because you care about your customer and want to be sure that understanding you is effortless. It is also a nice sign of generosity.

> Golden Rule Corner
>
> Be gentle in your communication: smile when you speak. It is another sign of a good education and also of self-confidence.

2.2.2 The Natural Posture

You need to remain natural, "very natural" should I say. It has to be you as a person, not a professional. You will give the impression that this is the way you communicate at the retail store, but also with friends or at home. Natural but also certainly with a "never too…" attitude: never speaking too quickly, too loudly, too long, too simple, too complicated, and never too much.

It best to speak naturally and fluidly but also in a rich, meaningful way. Speaking simply does not mean being simple, with only basic vocabulary. On the contrary: it is by being very precise and elegant that you can make the difference. But it should never be overdone.

2.2.3 Converse Rather Than Broadcast

Favor conversation mode rather than a broadcasting one: it is more comfortable for your customer and actually less energy expending for you. The best way to encourage your customer to speak is to leave some space! Pause after each sentence. Do not forget to smile nicely after every three sentences. You will be surprised: your customer is so eager to talk and to engage in conversation with you.

> Golden Rule Corner
>
> Only one person can speak at a time.
> Leave space for customers to speak!

A conversation is not a "monologue" nor a self-centric speech. Imagine that you go to a friend's place and he is only talking about himself and does not even listen and let you talk. Many sales advisors think it is good to speak about their brand and products with pride and love. Since brands call these people brand ambassadors or product experts, they feel that they have a first priority: to say as much as they can about what they know—sharing it all. Some advisors think that it is important to talk about themselves in order to establish personal relations and therefore they talk a lot. This approach only leads to a dead end. It is all about a subtle dosage of what you say yourself, and what space you leave to let a customer to express themselves, that the best sales advisors know how to control.

What you say is good but not the best thing. The most important thing is to answer perfectly the questions a customer might ask. Instead of telling all about the history of your brand sometimes it might be worth waiting a little. If the customer asks you how long your brand has been established, you are sure that what you say will be listened to and remembered.

Simon with Mrs. and Mr. Williams:
"Here we are! It's indeed a beautiful house."
"My work was to assist you in identifying this property and it's now up to you both!"
"Please tell me if there is anything you don't like—I will write everything down."

2.2.4   Be Precise

The products you are selling are full of detail and very precisely elaborated—whatever it is, whether a Luxury creation or a financial investment package. By being particular and precise in the words you are using, you will definitely illustrate the superiority of your products.

A pair of men's dress shoes? Let us be very precise. First they are characterized by the way they are fastened. They could be Oxford, Derby, a Monk's strap or slips-on. And they are also named as per their decoration (example: Brogue), the style (example: moccasin). By calling your product by the right word, you are already giving a clear message about the seriousness of your product and also your own professionalism.

> ### Manager's Corner
>
> Rework your team's vocabulary.
> There are always better ways to speak about your brand, products and services.

2.2.5   Enrich Your Vocabulary

Luxury selling means that your vocabulary should be rich, elegant and inspiring.

Martial with Mr. Peter Wang:
"Peter, I am very proud to submit my new timepiece for your appreciation. It's a grand complication deserving all your attention. Our creator decided on a very nice 18 K pink gold 4 N, and in an appropriate size of 42 mm, in a round-shaped case. The strap is in Louisiana midnight blue alligator, and of course hand stitched for the demanding collector such as yourself, Peter."

You can find appropriate vocabulary most of the time in internal documents or on corporate internet sites. But it is also worth looking in magazines, on competitors' website and so forth. The beginning point is to be curious, and to have a willingness to upgrade, to please, to seduce. Sometimes, by just looking at the brochures and catalogues that your company provides, you will already be able to find the different seductive terms that you could use.

2.2.6 Enlightening Your Expressions

A Luxury product and superior product cannot be just normal. They are always exceptional, amazing, extraordinary, incredible, absolutely delicious, awesome...

The best sales advisors have in their portfolio many expressions able to reflect positivity, joy and the pleasure of being in contact with these products. It is the privilege of being able to work with high-value creations and this has to be translated into the way sales advisor expresses themself.

Alice with Mrs. and Mr. Taylor:
"Madame, you look absolutely magnificent with this full-paved diamond necklace. It looks like it has been specially created for you. Simply extraordinary!"

2.2.7 Go Further

To self-improve, the best way is to listen to yourself.
Record yourself speaking about your products.
Are there words that you could upgrade? Do you have the right tone?
Are there any other possibilities to say the same things differently, in a nicer way?

Your words and expressions should reflect the image of the Luxury creations, in line with the high value products you are selling.

After looking Luxury, you prove you can be Luxury by the way you speak.

2.3   Luxury Gestures

Your image and language are just right. Now it is about gestures. The way you move in the store, how you sit, tells a lot about you. This also applies to your hands and the different, nicely controlled gestures that need to become part of your expression and will help your communication.

2.3.1 Be Aware and Keep Control

Every part of your body is able to move. It is possible to express things through movements and gestures. It is important to consider the impact of movements and gestures and to keep them under control. Let us look at this from head to toe:

Forehead:	Up, down movement
Eyebrows:	Up, down movement
Eyelids:	Blinking at different speeds
Eyeballs:	Up, down, right, left movement
Nose:	When breathing heavily
Ears:	Ability to move them is rare
Mouth/lips:	Very expressive
Tongue:	Movement inside the mouth can be seen
Shoulders:	Very expressive
Arms:	Very expressive
Hands:	Highly expressive true communication tool
Upper torso/waist:	Right, left movement
Stomach area:	When breathing heavily
Hips and legs:	Movement
Feet:	Movement

Your body expresses more than you think, and can betray you—dangerously. A raised brow usually indicates questioning, surprise or anger.

On the other hand, when gestures are mastered they reinforce your messages and empower your communication. After being conscious of what movements convey, you need to learn how to best control them.

Eyebrows: Can express surprise, but also negativity. Avoid moving them

Eyelids: Blink normally, avoid changes during the conversation

Eyeballs: Never look at customers sideways - sales advisors are not spies!

Nose: Some people tend to move their nose when they are nervous. Keep cool!

Ears: Some people's ears move when facing tense situations. Relax!

Mouth/lips: The rule is simple. Keep on smiling. What might change is the size of your smile, not the fact that you need to keep on smiling no matter what!

Tongue: Customers should never see your tongue protruding from your mouth for any reason. It's always a sign of poor education and bad manners.

Shoulders: They need to stay straight. Moving your shoulders up could be seen as aggressive. Moving them down would suggest a kind of tiredness or fatigue.

Arms: Keep them close to the body. Avoid big, scary, arm-waving gestures. Well mastered arm movements show that you are comfortable and the conversation is going well.

Hands: Hands are extremely expressive and many people (French, Italians) move hands naturally. Learning how to use your hands is essential. Open your palms, in a natural way, and avoid closing them. Always show both hands to your customers because this is reassuring. Moving hands gently is also sign of kindness.

Fingers: Fingers are there to help customers. And of course they should avoid all other activities!

Legs: Do not cross your legs even when you sit (it will be seen) and also because it will change the way you sit.

Golden Rule Corner
Express yourself through gestures by keeping control of the parts of your body that you can move.

As you can see, your body is part of your set of communication tools.

2.3.2 Be Graceful

The key word to describe Luxury selling gestures is grace. Being graceful first means that you apply the "never too" rule by always keeping your gestures tempered. They are never too big, never too fast—always steady. Grace comes from a combination of body languages. Just like for an actor or actress: the perfection in impersonation comes from a total control of all the details.

Try walking with a smile, at the right speed, with your arms moving gently and keeping a relaxed happy look on your face. Try sitting in front of your customer, speaking softly with a smile, moving your hands slowly while speaking and with charm in your eyes. Try taking a pen to write or draw an explanation for your customer. By holding a nice pen in an elegant way, writing slowly with fine penmanship, you show how much you care. All these details contribute to creating a very positive image and will put the customer at ease and make them feel special.

> ### Manager's Corner
> In the store, observe your store without listening (using, for example, earplugs). You will be surprised by all the gestures you see and will then be able to lead in effecting positive changes.

Martial Legrand could talk for a long time about the different gestures it is important to master:

- The way you walk into the boutique shows your personality
- The way your hold your watch shows your professionalism
- The way your use your hands to explain things shows your expertise
- The way you look at your customer shows your sincerity
- The way you help a customer to try on a watch shows your caring spirit
- The way you sit shows your respect of the client

2.3.3 Physical Contact: Handle with Care!

This is really a question of culture: your culture and the culture of your clients. It is also dependent upon the personality of the sales advisor and how the physical contact is executed. It can be sign of too much familiarity and therefore dangerous.

2.3.3.1   Shake Hands

In general, shaking hands is business-like, and mainly a Western gesture. I tend to recommend not shaking hands unless you are in more a business oriented or corporate environment, for example when selling a financial investment plan at an office. To shake hands is also commonly accepted so there is no real danger in offering to shake hands when you have a male customer visiting you. Of course, if you are receiving a couple and you shake hands with the husband be sure to not forget his wife. With Asian male customers, it is never a problem if you shake hands in a very natural way. It is more about how you shake hands than whether you should or not. I would never recommend shaking hands when a lady is visiting alone.

2.3.3.2   Touching Arms

This is to be reserved for family and friends and is to be avoided in a selling situation. It can be also perceived as a sign of domination. Even with a customer that you have known for a long time, I believe that some distance has to be kept.

2.3.3.3   Kisses and Hugs

Of course, this too should be reserved for family and friends, and mainly in the Western world.

Physical contact is sometimes very nicely executed and can increase closeness in a relationship. But as a rule, I would recommend avoiding physical contact and keep a necessary distance when you first meet someone. This is simply because physical contact is not necessary to succeed in sales and can be perceived as overly familiar, which is inappropriate. However, at the end of a customer visit, proposing to shake hands with your customer has a better chance of being perceived as appropriate and appreciated than at the beginning of the visit. A kiss to say goodbye and a hug would be appropriate only in exceptional circumstances.

Looking good, speaking nicely and with appropriate gestures: here you are ready for the next stage. To succeed in building Luxury interactions with your customer, you need to be a good person, "*une belle personne*" I would say in French. I invite you to be generous and care sincerely about your customer, as explained in the sections to follow.

Golden Rule

Always imagine you are on the stage, being watched.
You need to take possession of your own image.

Looking Luxury but also speaking Luxury with right gestures is crucial. Now you are ready to build Luxury interactions.

2.4   Building Luxury Interactions

Successful sales advisors are able to establish true and long lasting relationships with their clients. Moreover, they are able to set up, very quickly if not immediately, a quality customer relationship. They are necessarily outgoing, open, pleasant and charming. Going further than breaking the ice, the best advisors know how to "attract" (like a magnet) the customer to them.

This interaction has to be personal, sincere, friendly and caring.

2.4.1 A Personal Relation

The level of a personal relationship can be proportional to the value of the purchase. When you are at a fast food stand, the different menus are defined—you can only select few items. The ordering process is defined. Even your answers are set; it is mechanical and automatic. Let us study the differences between Luxury interactions and a fast food counter.

2.4.1.1   Taking Time

The first difference is the time factor. You need to take all the necessary time to allow a personal relationship to be able to develop. Customers always have time, even if they sometimes say they are in a hurry. You are never in a hurry if the service and the pleasure are there.

2.4.1.2   Being Spontaneous

Spontaneity makes a difference. Each customer is unique and deserves a different experience. Of course, sales advisors often have a well rehearsed selling "ceremony," or procedures to follow, but you should never look as if you are only executing preset processes as if you are working behind a fast food counter.

2.4.1.3 Ensuring The Human Touch

It is also necessary to show the human touch, which is mainly expressed through how you look at someone. Your natural smile, the care you take and the emotion you show. All these factors will resonate with your customer.

2.4.1.4 Establishing Personal Relations

To allow a personal relationship to develop, why not just make a simple greeting like:

Martial: "Sir, my name is Martial and I am the boutique director. Welcome! May I know how I can address you, Sir?"

Martial: "Mr. Wang, for your coffee, could you please tell me how you like it?"

Martial: "Mr. Wang, please do not hesitate to tell me your personal preferences and I will do my best to find the most appropriate offer for you."

The relationship is established quickly, with key words "you" and "me," in a polite and respectful way. A customer needs to know that you are also looking for that personal relationship.

2.4.2 Sincerity Of Regard

There is a Chinese saying that "the eyes are the window of the soul". That is why in many traditions, looking at someone straight in the eyes is the sign of trust. When you shake hands, when you toast, any important moment of commitment is accompanied with a frank, sincere exchange of looks.

The way you look, the expression on your face, says much more than you may be aware. When you are under stress (for example during a price negotiation), you look different and customers do see it! The same goes for your customers: there are many messages that you can "sense" coming from his or her look, especially the change of expressions that might occur.

Customers tend to not look at the sales advisor at the beginning of a visit. They generally only pay attention to the new environment (some boutiques might be intimidating) and the products. After some interaction, when the sales advisor is able to attract the customer's attention, then the customer might start to observe the sales advisor more seriously. It is only from that moment that the true interaction starts.

Not looking at your customer might be perceived as avoidance, escaping or not telling the whole the truth. Looking into their eyes has always been a sign of trust. The tradition of maintaining eye contact when you toast someone comes from medieval times.

Story Corner

In today's popular culture, looking someone in the eye when you say a toast, touching your glass to the other person's glass and then taking a first sip of a drink together, is a sign of good manners and upbringing. This was not the case in the Middle Ages when there was general paranoia about being poisoned. Guests at a banquet or celebration raised their cup or mug and banged it sufficiently hard against the cup of the other guest, so that their drink would slosh into the other person's cup on purpose. Then, they raised their cups to drink at the same time, while looking the other person straight in the eye, thereby proving that they had not poisoned the other person.

Staring at your customer is not friendly—it might be perceived too imposing, too aggressive. When you look at the customer, it has to be with a sincere look and with a true smile from the heart.

2.4.3 The Power Of A Friendly Smile

A first reason to smile: smiling is very pleasant for the one who smiles and also for the one who sees the smile. A sales advisor with a smile on his face tends to be more relaxed and more able to establish a quality, engaging relationship with clients and colleagues.

A smile is the true sign of an open attitude, expressed on the face. The eyes and the mouth show this open attitude. A smile is also the universal message of peace. It says to your customer: "I am a very nice person and I think that you are too."

A smile very often receives immediate reciprocity. It is difficult to not smile back at someone who just smiled at you.

A smile means pleasure. By showing that you interact with pleasure with your client, you are giving a nice compliment and are establishing a positive mood in the relationship.

A smile means self-confidence. Because you are relaxed, you look competent.

A smile is sign of strength. Leaders of the world smile, showing their teeth in a positive way. Facing an objection, a sales advisor that smiles gives the impression of someone with experience and able to handle the objection.

Are there times when you should not smile? Some argue that smiling can make sales advisors look less respectable, less professional. That might be true in business-to-business relationships. In retail, especially when there is a need to reassure, and the building of a quality relationship is key, I can only invite all sales advisors to practice giving a smile in a meaningful way, sincerely and from the heart.

> **Golden Rule Corner**
>
> Everyone shall smile, even to each other and not only to clients. Smiles are deliciously contagious.

2.4.4 A Caring Relation

A friend is someone who cares about you. More than just showing interest in your customer, try and really care about them. You will find that caring gestures help to quickly establish and solidify interaction so that a long-term relationship can develop and grow.

Henry: "Mr. Hudson, it's so hot outside today. You must be quite hot in a business suit. May I offer you a refreshment?"

Alice: "Mr. Taylor, Paris is my city and, please, if you need me to recommend restaurants, or if you have any specific requests, please just tell me!"

We will go into greater detail in the following sections, describing the spirit that will help you to succeed in acquiring this Luxury selling state of mind: be gentle, generous, human and professional.

2.5   Be Gentle

"*Gentillesse*" meaning kindness, is a very nice word in French.

A kind person is someone who cannot harm you. Providing services is not sufficient: service is expected and Luxury selling invites you to go beyond.

Story Corner

Franck is a sales advisor for a prestigious international men's luxury brand on New Bond Street. One day, a tourist from China was visiting his store. He was not very convinced by the made-to-order suits the brand was proposing and did not place any orders. Before leaving, the client asked him if he knew where to order bespoke suits in London. Franck took him, on his private time the next morning, to the different tailors on Savile Row. After visiting a few boutiques, the client asked Franck to go back to his boutique and placed the biggest single order of the year. "It's too complicated, he said to Franck. I have already found you—a good advisor—and I can be sure that my suits will be perfectly made!"

2.5.1   Respect Your Customer

The primary gentle gesture is about respect, so give full respect to your customer. It means that when your customer comes into your boutique or showroom for luxury cars, be sure to leave the necessary space and time. These gestures of respect are what your customer will expect from the best *maisons*.

When a customer comes in as a couple or as a family, be particularly sure to show respect to all of the family members. Look at and address all of the family members in the most courteous manner. Do not ignore any of them. If you take good care of the spouse, the child/children and all other family members, you can be sure that the senior customer in the family will not forget. If you take good care of any child in the family, you can be sure that the parents will appreciate it and will not forget your kind gesture.

Moreover, sometimes a customer comes into a store with assistants, body-guards or domestic helpers to mind their children. Do not hesitate to offer drinks to all and be sure to at least acknowledge their presence. Somehow, you have to thank them for being there, which will allow your customer to talk to you.

2.5.2 Helping Your Customer

Helping your customer is definitely the best way to show that you care. The best sales advisors have a real panoply of helpful tips and information resources, a sort of service tool box. It could be information which they have gathered, especially to help visiting tourist customers. Moreover, by anticipating all possible needs your visitors will be surprised by your kindness and also by your professionalism—being able to provide the extra mile in personal effort and special care is a very good thing. Some ideas are to provide:

- Maps of the city in different languages
- Shopping suggestions and tourism guidebooks
- Tax Free procedures in different languages

Some sales advisors even prepare custom made maps to guide their customers:

- New York City map of 5th Avenue showing the best restaurants
- Shopping tour with others brands and the best restaurants
- List of the best Chinese restaurants in London

Better yet, some sales advisors prepare personal guidance such as:

- A personal list of the preferred French restaurants in Paris' rue Saint-Honoré
- A personal list of the "real Italian" restaurants preferred by Italians in Milan

Helping is also the moment to establish a mutual relationship, not only one-way service. By accepting a service, your customer makes you happy. Why don't you just say it?

"I am here to help you! That is what me makes me happy!"
"Please let me assist you—you cannot imagine the pleasure I have in doing so."

2.5.3 A Gentle Place: Build Harmony

Customers coming to a store see it very quickly: it is in our instinct. When sales advisors are only there to sell, and at any price, they immediately feel it and walk away—escape. In the same way, customers feel very quickly when the store atmosphere is wrong: too much tension, no teamwork—an unhappy team will not produce a happy atmosphere for the boutique. Each sales advisor shall treat each colleague, from doorman to the tea lady the same way and as gently as possible. Smiling to each other is essential in a sales team, including always addressing each other by name and with the most elementary expressions of politeness: please and thank you.

> ### Manager's Corner
> Treat your team with *"gentillesse"* (kindness), and your team will treat your customers nicely. A gentle place is always made by the addition of happy and good hearts.

2.5.4 Protect Your Customer

A good friend cares about you, and will even protect you. There are various ways to show your customer that you are making an effort to protect him/her. A good sales advisor should never name-drop or mention any private data concerning his customers. Think about it—how can a customer trust you if are disclosing others clients' information? Protecting your customer also includes the way you care about customer security in general.

A first example is when a customer has to key-in the code for a credit card payment. Not only should the sales advisor avoid looking at the customer at this moment, but they should be sure to prevent any other customers possibly seeing the code. A customer's shopping bag, with a prestigious name on it, could become a security issue for some. Depending on the situation, it would make sense to propose covering the branded bag with a neutral bag, if the customer is going to spend the day touring in the city. Walking your customer to the taxi rank/stand or limousine is another simple protective gesture.

Especially nowadays, with all the security issues present in cities, customers will appreciate the different possible protections you could propose:

"Madam, would you like me to call our customer car to escort you to your hotel?"

"Madam, if you wish, I can also personally carry your bag directly to your hotel. I was thinking that you may not want to walk around Paris with too many things."

These caring gestures are always appreciated, whether the customer feels they need them, and accepts them, or not.

A strong sales advisor is not the one speaking the loudest. Being gentle is another sign of strength, as is the smile. It does not mean being weak. The best sales advisors have this inner self-confidence, expressed softly and sweetly.

The best gentle gestures are always the generous ones. By showing the highest respect to clients, my experience tells me that you will never be disappointed. More than immediate business, kindness often brings pleasant surprises. Reciprocity is part of human nature. By giving first, a sales advisor has more chance to receive in return than the one who is only thinking about immediate business.

2.6   Be Generous

A real friend respects you, helps you and even protects you. Better than that, he is someone who never hesitates to offer you gifts. These gifts might not matter in terms of value, but the way your friend has thought about them, and the way he delivers the gifts to you really counts!

2.6.1 Offer Without Expecting Things In Return

There are many ways to show generosity to a first-time visitor and to your regular customers.

Do not only promote: offer everything as a real gift. Sometimes a small gift is the nicest attention. In Paris, a sales advisor could have Metro tickets available in case a customer wanted to get to a place nearby and it was impossible to get a taxi (often the case in Paris). If it were convenient for the customer to get there by Metro, the tickets would be greatly appreciated and have great meaning. It could also be having some small, cute gifts for kids that you always have on-hand in case your customer comes to visit you with family. It could also be a selection of greeting cards, or classic stationary in case your customer has no time to get a card. The sales advisor, wherever possible, should have always small attentions to offer. The best is of course to offer a generous program proposed by your company when possible.

Simon:	"Mrs. and Mr. Williams, I would like offer you a one-day tour of Singapore to see some different places so that you have a first, but good idea of the city."
Mr. Williams:	"That's very nice of you. We just don't want to bother you."
Simon:	"Actually I will not be able to do it but I have students helping out on this program."
Mrs. Williams:	"Thank you for this nice proposal of a tour, that would definitely be welcome."
Simon:	"Don't feel obliged to commission my agency. It is all part of the Singapore hospitality we like to promote."
Mr. Williams:	"I hope we will not make you lose your lunch break because of us."
Simon:	"Sir, the most important thing is that you know our city before selecting the place you want to visit. We are happy that we have the chance and privilege to be the first to introduce to you our city."
Mrs. Williams:	"That's so sweet."

Of course, a gift does not mean immediate returns on investment. It is more an open door for further discussions, and provides a trust that money cannot buy.

2.6.2 Everyone Likes Good Surprises!

When you are a high-tier customer for an international hotel chain, upon arrival at the hotel you tend to receive a welcome letter, a welcome fruit basket, wine and other nice items of attention. Most frequent travelers do not pay attention to, or even read, the letter from the hotel manager. This is simply because such special attention is expected and no longer considered to be part of the magic of Luxury travelling. Surprising your client is the best way to create difference and be remembered.

Story Corner

In Thailand, I stayed at the Mandarin Oriental Bangkok. In the morning, I asked for a French newspaper in the breakfast restaurant, knowing that there was little chance they would have one. Surprisingly, the restaurant asked me to wait and called the concierge to come. The concierge kindly asked me which newspapers I needed and also informed me that he needed about ten minutes to get them, if that would be fine with me. I was very impressed and asked the Hotel Director how they managed to provide such a large selection of international titles? "Well," he said, "we just send our bellboy to get them at the nearest international newsagent." The nice surprise was that next day, these titles were waiting for me at the restaurant, without my asking. I asked the director again: "What would have happened if I had not come to breakfast?" He answered, "we would have sent them to your room. This is the nicest surprise we can provide to you."

Surprise your customers! When you remember an anniversary and send a gesture on that day it is a very nice thing. But your customer might well already have received many gestures on that day. What about if you send a gesture two weeks before the anniversary and tell them that you remember that it is in two weeks' time? Then you would be the first and the customer will remember.

Your customer mentioned his love for chocolate? Prepare few pieces for her or him from a *chocolatier* you really like for the next visit.

2.6.3 Offer The Extraordinary

The best thing is to be able to provide an extraordinary surprise that your customer will remember forever. It is often found in the services, the experience, more than an expensive gift that you or your company might be able to offer. With creativity and your desire to please, you will be able to achieve and find the way to make the difference. Doing what everyone is doing is seen as normal. Proposing in a better way, what is offered by others is good: you are more sophisticated. Offering what has never seen is showing you are able to really care.

When we deal with affluent customers in particular, they can be bored and will have already been in all kinds of places and seen what they need to see. So, try simple things: a small piece of artisanal jewelry, personalized with your customer's children's names; a small book that you are sure your customer would love to read. It is all about that extraordinary attention, and never about the value of such things.

In Paris, introduce them to the secret French restaurants. In London, know some places that your customer has surely never been to and that are really worth a visit.

Story Corner

Franck is a sales advisor in Taiwan, for one of the most reputed and prestigious car brands. When he learned that world-class magician, David Copperfield was coming to Taipei for the first time he proposed and got approval from his management for an extraordinary gift to his best clients. He offered to take their kids and only the kids to the show. He organized transportation pick-up, snacks during the intermission and photo souvenirs. How could these customers go to another sales advisor when Franck treated their kids so well?

And I nearly forgot the true pleasure of generosity. We all remember our immediate feeling after helping someone, especially someone you do not know and are not obliged to help. It is an immense pleasure. When you give without return there is an immense joy to be had. You will be happy that day. You are making someone's day, but also your own!

2.7   Be Caring

Let us keep imagining the best possible friend. It is a person you can trust, a person who tells you the truth. A sincere person gives you a most precious gift: his true heart. It is also a friend who is able to understand you as yourself. Last but not least, it is someone who really cares about your feelings.

2.7.1 Sincerity: Stay Honest

As a sales advisor, you certainly have sales objectives and need to sell. But this does not prevent you from always being honest. A sales advisor does not lie simply because lying is sometimes easy, although obviously it can be dangerous. Sincerity comes from the Latin "*sincerus*," meaning pure, unmixed, genuine. It is because you are yourself, not pretending to be someone you are not, that your customer can feel that you deserve his trust. Faking does not stand up against time: your customer will see it. It's always better to be natural, simply yourself.

Story Corner

King Henry asked three of his best chevaliers to come to him at his castle.
"If you are loyal to me," he said, "you will always carry out what I ask you to do."
He asked them to come near to the window and said:
"If I want you to jump out of this window, will you do it?"
The first chevalier said "Yes, my King, I will without hesitation, even if I die."
"Liar," said King Henry.
The second chevalier said "Yes, my King, I will, even if I am not ready to die."
"Liar," said King Henry.
The third said "Yes, my King, I will. It's high but there is still a chance that I will survive."
"Voilà!" said King Henry and added: "Sincerity is a virtue."

2.7.2 Empathy: Assume Your Customer's Position, Really Understand

Empathy is defined as "the feeling that you understand and share another person's experiences and emotions: the ability to share someone else's feelings." Empathy is a true quality of a caring person. It means that you can forget about your position and put yourself in the position of the customer. By doing this, you will be able to see things that you might not able to spot otherwise, by staying in your own position. It is definitely a quality of the best sales advisors.

This is about being humble: you might not always be right and your customer might have a different point of view that you need to anticipate and listen to. You will be able to see more clearly and anticipate things if you are able to genuinely put yourself in your customer's position. The more effort you place in being empathic, the easier it will become, and the more capable you will become in bringing new convincing elements into the conversation.

In order to adopt an empathic position during a sales conversation, forget about your sales objectives for a moment. Your willingness to achieve your selling goal might make you forget about the present motivation and state of mind of your customer. While you are making your sales pitch, can you imagine that your customer has decided to not to buy? Immediately ask yourself, for example, are you proposing the correct product?

If your customer seems to appreciate the product, consider if there are still factors that are not right. What are they?

Your customer seems to have a desire for the product, but he still has fears that are keeping him from taking the decision to purchase. What are they?

Ask yourself, as if you were the customer: what are all my concerns about the product?

Manager's Corner

Encourage a culture based on empathy. The key question to ask is: "If you were the customer, what would you say or how would you feel?"

2.7.3 Sympathy: Be Able To Really Care About Your Customer

What if you have a friend who feels what you feel, and is sorry about your trouble, grief or misfortune? Sympathy comes from the Greek words, *"Sym"* meaning sharing and *"Pathos"* meaning feelings. Sympathy is not only being able to feel the same feelings as someone else: it is a true feeling of caring.

As a customer, if you sense that your sales advisor can feel what you feel, you are reassured. You feel that you are cared for, whatever might happen.

"Love Your Customer"

In speaking about customer relations in different countries during training sessions, it is remarkable how sales advisors react differently when I say: "Love Your Customer." In Europe, most sales advisors find it meaningless. "You don't need to love your customer," some even replied. "What you need to do is provide the best services to your client and be sure that you are able to develop an excellent relationship with your clients" would be the general comment.

In Asian countries, most of sales advisors agree with this comment: "Of course, you need to be truly sincere towards your customer and love your customer." When the relationship is based on true feeling, it is easier to sell.

In Japan, most of the time I did not receive any comment at all on this statement. For them, it was completely obvious that a good sales advisor would "love their customer." After all, love also means respect, devotion and commitment.

Story Corner

My mother used to have a small costume jewelry boutique in Paris. One of the clients became a regular. Josiane enjoyed coming to the boutique a lot, having conversations with my mother and always ended up buying things. One day, when Josiane wanted to buy a new piece of jewelry, my mother told her to not do it. Josiane was surprised and asked why. "You have already a lot of jewelry and you don't always need to buy something when you come here for a coffee." Josiane kept coming for a chat once a week. "I cannot let her buy so much," my mother told me "because now I know her stories and she had better save money at this moment." Luxury relationships are about true generosity.

2.8   Build Competency

When we qualify a sales advisor as "competent" we simply mean that they have the ability to sell. In fact, more than that, it implies that the sales advisor is able to sell well—even very well—to different kinds of customers and is able to adapt to various sales situations.

The ability to adapt to various situations is the reason that some sales advisors are consistently more able to close successful sales, and not because they are lucky and always have easier customers.

This ability is made up of what we called the components of competency:

– Knowledge (product, industry, customer)
– Know-how (selling techniques)
– Knowing how to behave (behavior)

Having knowledge without selling skills is just information, and not very useful in a selling situation. But a sales advisor who has selling skills but not the product or market knowledge is not professional. With both knowledge and know-how, the best sales advisor is the one who has the best attitude for selling.

A competent sales advisor is able to sell in any situation. They are more consistent in realizing sales. It is not because they are lucky and always have easier customers. The competence (also commonly called experience) makes the difference.

2.8.1   Knowledge (information)

As a professional dealing with high value items, luxury sales advisors certainly have to know their own brand perfectly: products, prices and the services provided. Moreover, an experienced sales advisor needs to have general knowledge about his industry and the main competitors: comparable brands, competitive products, price differences with competition and services available in the market. It is easy to get a sense and take the temperature of what customers think by logging in to blogs and forums.

There are so many simple ways to get and improve knowledge. A first simple tip is to take all the necessary time to carefully read all brochures, catalogs and the internet sites of your brand and that of the competition. Most of the time, rich and qualitative information is easily available. A second tip is to do extensive research.

You will be amazed by the quantity of information provided by extraordinarily generous and knowledgeable persons online, posting and sharing their passion.

Knowledge will make you feel powerful and fearless in your selling activity.

2.8.2 Know-How (selling techniques)

A sales advisor who is knowledgeable and has good selling techniques tends to feel more powerful and fearless in daily selling. This is particularly the case when a sales advisor has a selling plan—what some Luxury brands call a selling ceremony or the art of selling. I prefer to keep talking about selling techniques—applying this terminology to all the different aspects we discuss in this book.

> *Story Corner*
>
> *At a dinner grouping the best 3-star Michelin chefs, these top chefs discussed culinary art and, notably, the importance of a recipe.*
>
> *"Having a recipe is one of the fundamentals of our art," one chef said "because if you put everything in writing, and very precisely, you can be sure that the results will always there!"*
>
> *Another top chef disagrees: "Well, my recipes are not as precise as I might be. How to be precise when each time, there is something changing and adaptations are necessary? I give a road map but never a program for execution to my deputy chef!"*
>
> *A third chef has another opinion: "Anyway, even you have the most precise of recipes, but subtle additions and modifications are needed during cooking, if your deputy chef does not know how to achieve each step of your recipe, your recipe is in vain."*
> *A last chef concluded neatly: "Well, at least we all agree that there is no good chef without recipes and appropriate techniques."*

Know-how for selling is the essence of your *métier*, your pride. Sometimes, sales advisors are so adept at selling that when they sell, they always follow a selling flow—we can see it in the selling process. In the final chapter, we will extensively review the seven steps of this proven successful selling process:

– Preparation
– Welcoming
– Discovering
– Presenting
– Convincing

– Concluding
– Loyalty building

Some sales advisors just sell so naturally that they forget that they have, and use selling techniques, tricks that they employ during the selling process. We will add to the techniques in their portfolio and enrich the process with new ideas, offering different ways to approach and tackle selling situations.

Know-how makes you feel confident and helps you to master all selling situations.

2.8.3 Knowing How To Behave (attitude)

At the start of this book I discussed sales advisors extensively:

– How to look Luxury: to be remarkable
– How speak Luxury: to set your conversation at a Luxury level
– How adopt Luxury gestures: to be graceful

And also I invited you to be as generous as possible. Be gentle, caring about your customer; you will surely be rewarded.

This knowledge is easy to acquire, and it is possible to learn good selling techniques. What will really make the difference is your selling behavior.

You will make the difference because you are able to inspire and develop and keep a long-term relationship going by truly caring about your customer.

> Golden Rule Corner
>
> Being knowledgeable and skillful makes you a professional.
> Your behavior is what makes your selling, Luxury selling.

2.8.4 Decide The Changes For Yourself

I invite you to do a simple exercise. Please think about yourself, inspired by this chapter, and ask what you could you do to keep on improving? Write around ten "post-it" notes outlining the different changes that you want to realize for yourself, such as:

– *Adopt light and subtle make-up*
– *Adopt wearing a tie and pocket square*

— Celebrate my top ten customers' birthdays
— Find small gifts for kids and be ready to give them out

Place your post-its at the end of this book. When you have finished the book, look at them again. How many of the actions have been realized?

To develop your own competence, you need first to think about the three components of this competence:

Knowledge; know-how; knowing how to behave

Now you not only need to learn and accumulate knowledge, but also accept the importance of developing your own skills. I encourage you to change, in order to adopt the right attitude. And with the right attitude, you will have the self-learning spirit.

This is what I call the virtuous circle of the selling competence development (Chart 2.1).

To be Luxury is the first step in Luxury selling. Only if you have this mindset will you be able to succeed. I believe that then you truly understand your own power to influence your customers.

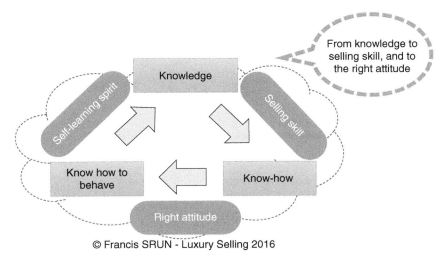

© Francis SRUN - Luxury Selling 2016

Chart 2.1 Competence development dynamic

2.8.5 Learning By Experimentation

To really learn and acquire true competence I invite you to experiment. This is a self-explanatory selling competence development program. There is no acquisition and consolidation of knowledge and selling skills without experimentation. In the same view, you only learn the right attitude by practicing it (Chart 2.2).

> *Golden Rule Corner*
>
> The more you sell, the more you know how to sell.

In the next chapter we are going to talk about who is in front of you: your Luxury clients. We will give you insightful information about them: who they are, why they buy Luxury. I will walk you through the different types of international clientele, and elaborate more extensively about Chinese luxury clientele.

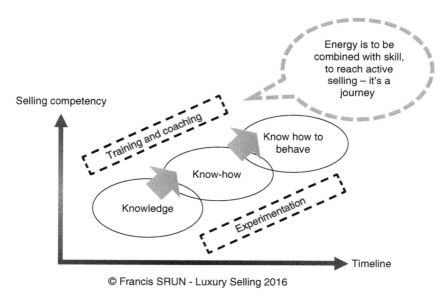

© Francis SRUN - Luxury Selling 2016

Chart 2.2 Competence building dynamic

3

Luxury Customer's Decision Process

3.1   Understanding Luxury

Luxury selling is firstly about selling Luxury creations. You certainly want to know why your clients buy, or even need to buy, Luxury creations. Let's firstly consider what Luxury is.

Luxury for many people means unnecessary, in the sense that the items have no real utility. Luxury for many people implies the unaffordable: "this is not for me."

On the other hand, Luxury always offers the feeling of pleasure, of a treat or an experience. Luxury is about quality.

> **Story Corner**
>
> Allan Williams arrives at one of the finest hotels in Singapore with his wife Sophie. Upon their arrival, the Guest Manager greets them at the taxi, addressing Allan by name. Allan is surprised; he wonders how the Manager knew when they were arriving since Allan had chosen to travel by taxi rather than use the hotel's limousine. Allan's room is, of course, ready and the Guest Manager escorts them directly to it, for a fast and discreet check-in. Even as a frequent business traveler, Allan is impressed and very much appreciates this personal touch of luxury.
>
> At the hotel's award-winning French restaurant, a couple are celebrating their 20th wedding anniversary. They hadn't celebrated their 10th anniversary; financially, it was not an easy time back then. Today, they really want to have a

F. Srun, *Luxury Selling*, DOI 10.1007/978-3-319-45525-9_3

memorable evening, a truly luxurious one. Allan and Sophie also decide to have dinner there—a quick dinner before going to sleep.

An American Hollywood star, Johnny, has also decided to stay at the same hotel with his family. He has made sure that he is able to enjoy a simple and discreet stay at the hotel. No press, no admirers—just a family getaway. The true luxury for Johnny is to let his children live like other people's kids do: with their parents, enjoying simple and quality family time. They ask the French restaurant to send some pancakes for the kids—that's the real treat.

Luxury is always about experience. Allan and Sophie's check-in is magical. How was this achieved? It was not the probable five minutes of time saved by bypassing the reception desk that was particularly agreeable to Allan. It was the personal touch. He suspected that this amazing welcoming was not a coincidence and must be quite something to organize. In fact, the reception team had to make sure to have the customer data and flight details and be particularly organized. The secret tool was the luggage team who are trained to spot bags to find names and to identify guests upon arrival. The Hospitality Manager is on stand-by to check if the guest is on the VIP list. Allan and Sophie have the assurance that the hotel will do all that is necessary to make their stay a pleasant one. A simple check-in becomes a magic show—memorable.

Luxury is not simply about money. It's also about the quality of the time, product and services that we experience. The experience of the hotel's French restaurant could represent either a Luxury offer or just a quick bite. The true Luxury for Allan and Sophie was the magical and surprising welcoming experience. The true Luxury for the couple celebrating at the French restaurant was the decision to be together for a memorable supper. And true Luxury for Johnny was to be with his family, and only his family.

There are different kinds of Luxury. Luxury is not about utility or functionality. It is not always about money. It is about quality and pleasure. It is about experience and appreciation. It is something exceptional, an escape from daily life that we always appreciate. And we all have our own idea of luxury.

3.1.1 Luxury Goes Beyond Simple Functionality

A handbag could be considered a necessity but it does not have to be made of alligator skin or leather. It could just be made of fabric. It does not need to have a good design or be in a beautiful color. Who needs a wristwatch to read time when we all have a mobile telephone? What about the accuracy of mechanical timepieces? They are not particularly precise—even the most expensive ones are less precise than the time displayed on a cellphone! The first important idea to grasp is that Luxury goes beyond functionality—it has more to offer.

To be more precise, a Luxury creation is a superior product. It therefore utilizes advanced technology and is more durable than other items—and it offers increased functionality. The value of such a creation depends on whether you appreciate this added value.

3.1.2 Luxury Is Necessarily Qualitative

The quality implies research, an effort to make something better. A handbag in fabric is sufficient but when it is in leather, it is most likely to be more durable, more substantial. When in alligator skin (the most durable material), it can last indefinitely. A fabric Luxury bag would most likely be in a certain type of fabric, for example a strong canvas to give it weight and structure and it may be treated to be durable and even stain resistant. Brands are always innovating and researching in the quest for better quality in order to deliver a superior product. Of course, not everyone needs a higher level of quality. For customers of Luxury brands, quality is important, if not essential. They are often very demanding in their professional capacity, or in their private life. They feel that they deserve the same level of quality in everything they use, eat, buy and so on.

3.1.3 Luxury Is About Pleasure

Of course, not everyone needs or appreciates owning an alligator-skin handbag. Some would very much appreciate the beauty of the material, with its beautiful, proportional scales. These customers probably like the feel of the skin: solid, reassuring and warm. Firstly, there is the beauty of the product—what we can call the aesthetic. There is pleasure in handling a superior Luxury product and even in the smell of the luxury leather of an alligator skin handbag. For those who invest in such Luxury items, the belief is that life is not simply about sustenance. When eating, everyone prefers good food. Why not trying having the best?

3.1.4 Luxury Is About The Long Term, and Sustainability

Luxury creations are made to last. A piece of jewelry is passed down from mother to daughter. Particularly when the item is made of gold or precious stones, they are designed to last for generations, if not forever. A beautiful piece of jewelry is always memorable—just like a wristwatch that a father would pass on to his son. It's not only about the monetary value, but the emotional value—what it represents.

Some customers may prefer to purchase new products and change them more often. Most clients of Luxury items would think longer term. Since I need to acquire a product, it has to last. The design should be timeless— quality never fades—and the customer needs to be able to continue to derive pleasure from it, liking it forever.

A product of excellent quality is durable. For many customers, it is often the "I buy less but better" attitude, which is definitely a positive mindset in terms of sustainability. It could be therefore a gentle reminder to a customer that the decision is wise because it is good to "buy less but better." It's a buying mindset to encourage.

But sustainability is not only about "buying less but better." It's an overarching awareness that includes nature protection, environment preservation, fair trade, natural replacing chemical, animal rights and many other concerns.

At present, customers do not expect to buy only sustainable Luxury products. It's more a "quality product first" attitude with clients as with the majority of brands. Many initiatives are from unique brands that are increasingly conscious about, and willing to be part of, the need for sustainability. Can a product qualify as good—a precious creation that is supposed to last—when it contributes to the destruction of the planet? Can a precious creation be appreciated by one person but considered unethical for another? Can a brand claim to be the best in its category yet be damaging the environment (remember the provenance of the raw materials)? Can a brand talk about heritage while damaging the future of humanity?

There are more and more concerns, especially among the younger generations, about environmental responsibilities, as well as social responsibilities. The concern for product sustainability will definitely increase for Luxury items just like for others products. And, from the customer point of view, high value brands need to be at able to demonstrate and embrace these responsibilities. Luxury and high priced items will have no choice and cannot disappoint.

It's important for sales advisors to be aware of this sustainability tidal wave—and to pay attention to all possible sustainability initiatives from brands, manufacturers and retailers. It is important to understand and to learn about what it means to be sustainable, and what you can say about the issue when customers put forward their concerns about sustainability.

3.1.5 Luxury Is Always Emotional

Luxury is not simply functional; it is necessarily emotional.

The first aspect of emotion is evidently the brand. A brand is a concentration of emotional resonance. Why does this brand speak to me rather than another one? Why do I feel that this brand is more "me" and I cannot stand this other brand? Each brand has its own heritage, values (subtlety communicated) and image. And brands have a notoriety which lends them the power of being in the public eye, having star quality. Luxury brands are therefore able to provide this emotional resonance: I am buying a brand that is really me and somehow I am part of this brand.

Secondly, the heritage and tradition of a brand play a very important role in the imagination of the customer. The heritage reflects what is authentic and what cannot be changed or questioned: the past. The heritage of a brand is unique (impossible to reproduce), strong and has authority. Some customers feel that they become part of this tradition by being able to own one of the creations from that legacy.

The third aspect of the emotional value is that offered by the product itself. It could be about the design—the aesthetic, the wonderful creation that I had always anticipated, the one that speaks to me. This artistic appreciation varies, and most likely explains why we have such variety in Luxury creations.

We will discuss shortly the power of the brand.

3.1.6 Luxury Is Not About Price

You might be surprised by the fact that I had not yet mentioned anything about price. A high price tag is simply related to the product itself. A handbag could be expensive due to the material and the craftsmanship needed to make it. But consider the possible variations between alligator skin handbags of the same size. The Luxury handbag is the one that is able to go beyond functionality (and not only durability), providing the highest quality compared to other alligator skin handbags (in terms of the quality of the leather, the crafting and the execution of the details), being long lasting and achieving emotional resonance with clients.

Luxury selling involves customers not being afraid of a highly priced item, but being part of this qualitative, long-term approach toward Luxury creations and their proposal.

3.1.7 Luxury Is Relative

Last but not least, Luxury to one person might not be the same to another. Likewise, what might not seem to be Luxury to someone could be Luxury to many others.

Affluent clients could be immensely wealthy. Some buy Luxury items quite simply because they only buy high-end products. It is not about showing off, to put it bluntly. For some clients, it is about affirming a lifestyle, and nothing more. It is about supporting heritage and tradition.

Some clients have to save money to afford an exceptional treat and deserve all the respect. Let's recognize that there is some possible desire for quality and pleasure from time to time for all of us.

Some clients are particularly sensitive and truly appreciate design, quality and craftsmanship. Luxury creations and high quality items are carefully crafted and create real appreciation.

There are different types of Luxury just as there are different consumer profiles. I will explain other characteristics of Luxury customers, notably values and needs, such as "self-affirmation" and hedonism.

Thinking Corner

What is your Luxury today?

Santa Claus is still in your heart. He is willing to offer you a Luxury product or service. What would it be?

3.2   Self-Affirmation

Luxury has always existed, in various forms, throughout history. Luxury corresponds to a human aspiration—the need for self-affirmation.

It translates into different aspects:

- The search for self-esteem
- The eagerness for success
- Social accomplishment
- The expectation of rewards
- The need for pleasure

Most of the consumers of Luxury and high-end value products are self-made men and women, notably within the new economy (the internet) and "emerging" markets such as China, India and Thailand. These consumers evidently have a very different relation with the idea of success and money.

There are common values around success that are shared worldwide. This is a triumph of the liberal system's values: everyone can succeed and success today is mainly expressed in new business (such as new e-ventures) and international expansion. Successes are possible and happen increasingly often; fast success is taking place in all kinds of business. I want it; I can; I made it; I deserve it.

3.2.1 Need For Self-Esteem

We all need success and we need self-esteem. Self-esteem gives us more self-confidence and reduces fear. A person with self-esteem engages better socially and tends to be in a position of leadership. Most wealthy and affluent customers have worked hard to succeed. They might not need you to increase their self-esteem but buying Luxury creations and high value products is an aspect of their self-esteem. Recall:

Alice: "It's not about the price of the jewelry, Madame, and I am sure that your husband agrees with me. It's the symbol of his appreciation for being with you for over twenty years. And you certainly deserve such a beautiful present!"

3.2.2 Eager For Success

From the beginning of our school life there is the need to succeed—in our studies, in assessments and in rankings. We work hard because we are encouraged and required to succeed. Customers, just like everyone else, need to triumph.

For many customers, being able to own a handbag from a high-end brand is a sign of success—being able to consume high priced products. Of course, as discussed, a customer buys an alligator skin handbag for the quality but also certainly with the idea that having a high-end branded alligator skin bag represents success.

It is therefore important to highlight customers' success. And there is always success to celebrate with clients. Recall Michelle and her husband in Paris. Their sales advisor, Alice, is able to emphasize the couple's success.

The key words on which to capitalize could be success, achievement, goals reached and so on.

"It's such a wonderful and important moment, Madame."
"It's a success to celebrate your 20th wedding anniversary!"
"And you both make such a lovely couple!"

Story Corner

Peter Wong is a frequent traveler. He has already reached the highest status with his favorite company. At the first class check-in counter from Hong Kong to Paris, the stewardess proposed to upgrade him from business class to first class. Moreover, she walked from behind the counter to greet Peter and congratulated him on behalf of the air company for his amazing achievement in reaching 2 million miles. She proposed to have a flight attendant escort Peter through the VIP channel which was already organized. On the plane, Peter received a card, written by the captain, congratulating him for his achievement and that the mileage makes him one of the most exclusive passengers. The service in first class was exceptional, but moreover, what Peter remembers most was the different gestures—which were, by the way, not so expensive for the company to provide.

3.2.3 Social Accomplishment

We can obtain self-confidence with better self-esteem—the true sentiment of success. We can also be proud of being recognized by others. We live with others and our own perception of ourselves depends on how others perceive us. That perception of ourselves gives us further self-confidence which is passed on and creates motivating Managers who are offering even more growth potential to their team members. It is also important to encourage customers and motivate them positively. You are part of their social accomplishment.

Alice:
"And you certainly deserves such a beautiful present!
I am sure that all your friends will be so happy for you, seeing you wearing such a nice present from your husband!"

Brands also allow for social recognition; owning certain brands invokes meaning. Brands have a certain social image and perception and contribute to building the owner's social image. This is the "aura" effect: the customer benefits from the positive image and associations of the brand.

Mrs. Taylor when considering the purchase might look for these aspects of social recognition:

"I love this necklace. I'm not really looking for a necklace that everyone will recognize."
"I will wear this necklace at our party. It will be noticed, right?"

The key words to which customers are sensitive are accomplishment, exceptional, extraordinary, great social contribution and so on.

– *"You made it!"*
– *"You have accomplished so many things."*
– *"What you did is just exceptional."*
– *"What you achieved is really extraordinary."*

There are always customer accomplishments that can be congratulated. It is up to you to identify these accomplishments, and be nice enough to acknowledge them. Sales advisors should become part of the social recognition process.

3.2.4 The Expectation Of Rewards

When we were young, we received rewards for our efforts at school: a picture, a book, a diploma. These rewards are important to us; they are part of our education. Later in our professional lives, we are concerned with performing, to earn a promotion (work recognition), a pay rise (financial reward), a management role (social power reward) and responsibility (leadership reward).

We need these rewards—it is human nature to want to progress, especially in the first active period of our lives. These rewards are a way for us to keep moving and progressing to a better life which we are all looking for. Being rewarded is part of our expectations.

Alice:
"You deserved it, and I am sure that you and your husband worked hard to reach the accomplishments you have today!"
"Madame, it's about the great feeling your husband has for you!"

We can also choose to self-reward. Our Luxury customers are affluent; they worked hard to reach their level of wealth. They also need to receive rewards along the way. Many of them are self-employed—business owners. They simply need to reward themselves from time to time. Self-rewarding is also part of their work–life balance.

Alice:
"The necklace is a symbol of these years together—precious, marvelous, magical".
"I am sure you both treasured these years together, and here is the crown of your union!"

The key words to focus on are joy, pleasure and happiness.

3.2.5 It Is Always About Self-Affirmation

Recall from Chapter 1, Mark who ran the New York marathon. This was probably a self-affirmation decision, a challenge to himself that he can make it (the time he took to run it doesn't matter).

Peter, as a watch collector, prides himself in being one the most knowledgeable "*haute horlogerie*" lovers (not for having the largest collection). Paul is looking for financial protection for his family; he wants to take a protective decision for his family, as a father and a husband (it's not only about the yield of the financial product).

Self-affirmation is positive. It is about ego but not only about ego. We can also see it as a positive aspect in life. It's about me but not only me. It is a success that I have worked hard for and that I am sharing with others.

Here you see that we have started our journey into the customer's psychology. We will keep on exploring, and together identify how, by understanding their psychology better, we can improve service and the Luxury experience for wealthy customers.

3.3 Pleasures

3.3.1 Needed Pleasures

Story Corner

In their book *Poor Economics*, the two economists Barnajee and Duflot reported their studies of the consumption habits of poor families in India. The biggest challenge to development is always education, especially the education of girls. The lack of financial resources was always the reported as the reason that poor families do not send their daughters to school. The claim has always been if they had more money, they would certainly be able to provide access to education for all their children equally. To test this claim, extra income was given to poor families and the research challenge was to determine what percentage of the extra income these families would actually devote to educating their children. Social workers noticed that instead of devoting all the extra income to the education of the children, a large part of the income went to purchasing some comfort foods and items, including cigarettes. It was found that when the households had more income, they would get a cellphone and even a television set, instead of saving all the money for the education of their children.

The search for pleasure is part of human nature, as discussed in the previous section. Somehow, it's also in our nature to consume now and not save for later or, worse, tomorrow. Why save for later when you can enjoy something in the here and now? It is also proven that humans tend to seek pleasure, and without pleasure people have less motivation and less energy. Our wealthy clients are no different, and mentioning pleasure will trigger another aspect in the decision making process.

In Western culture pleasure is not always a word associated with virtue. This is sometimes owing to religion and cultural background; it is not necessarily the case in other cultures. Why feel bad when you have the possibility to please yourself and offer agreeable experiences and incredible gifts to your loved ones?

Lisa Lam did not need another bag. She just feels that she deserves that pleasure, having not bought a new bag for some time—how long exactly she isn't sure. In her stressful working life with its worldwide traveling, being able to allow herself a treat from time to time, to purchase the unnecessary, is part of her requirement for pleasure and reward.

3.3.2 Pleasure Of Self-Affirmation

As discussed in the previous section, being able to self-affirm and to self-accomplish is part of human nature. It is important as a social being to be able to be perceived in the eyes of others as being of value and having a social value.

It is a pleasure to be able to be the person you want to be. In Chapter 1 we saw that Paul Morgan wanted a premium Luxury car. This is what he always imagined that one day he might be able to achieve. The car is not only a status item. It represents self-affirmation that he managed to achieve his goals. And, why not?

The pleasure from this self-affirmation is also evident with Mrs. and Mr. Taylor when looking for a piece of jewelry to celebrate their 20th wedding anniversary. There may not be many occasions for Michelle to wear this jewelry. It will most likely be kept in a safe. But it symbolizes something beyond the purchase of diamonds. It is about a celebration of their love, the material representation of the days spent together and those to come.

3.3.3 Pleasure Of The Best

Many products, with their ever better quality, are created to please us in order to answer our need to enjoy products of a superior quality. A 3-star Michelin restaurant will certainly not only feed you, but will also create culinary emotion. It is an extraordinary pleasure to experience how food can be so enjoyable and reach such a high standard. It is a pleasure that certainly only a few can afford. If you have the financial means, would you like to try it? After you had tasted it, would you like to taste it again?

It is not always about money. It is about the pleasure of having the best—the desire experience something that is pleasing to our senses. It is about education refinement and sensibility.

Peter Wang has always being fascinated by mechanics. He likes the idea of searching for perfection. His collection of timepieces reflects this constant search for the best. It is not about showing off but about the self-confidence of someone who can access and knows how to discern the best. Incidentally, Peter never displays his collection—other than to those who also appreciate timepieces.

Key phrases to use with customers could be:

– *"You really know how to appreciate the best."*
– *"You really know how to appreciate the best of the best!"*
– *"You do have very discerning taste."*

3.3.4 Pleasure Of Power

Clearly, not everyone can afford to enjoy highly priced Luxury creations. Not everyone can buy a nice property by the beach. Being able to afford these products provides customers with a sense of power.

Some customers can afford products without any cost limitations, and at any time. It is nothing more than a freedom they enjoy. And it is usually carried out without arrogance but also without any guilt. It is for some of us like being able to buy a new pair of sneakers without too much hesitation. Some affluent customers are able to purchase products a thousand times more expensive—also without hesitation—because they hold this financial power.

Phrases to acknowledge this situation could be:

"You surely could, especially if you really wanted to!"
"I am sure that you can take this decision."
"The most important factor is whether you like it or not."

Story Corner

When I was a student at MIT, I benefited from a scholarship. It included, I remember, free tuition and came with around US$ 500 in monthly subsidies, which was sufficient for me to live on and devote myself entirely to my computer *science studies. The different companies I created were very successful, and I became a millionaire without being conscious of my wealth. My family and I have a very comfortable life. I did not realize the meaning of my wealth until I took the most important decision of my life so far. I decided to donate US$ 5 million to MIT. I did this out of gratitude. But I found that this decision also brought me more than I gave. I felt for the first time that the money in my bank account could be useful to others. I felt powerful and there is an immense pleasure related to this. This is my true luxury.*

3.3.5 Pleasure Of The Relationship

Even as a billionaire, you cannot afford everything. What you will appreciate the most, is what money cannot buy. It's about health, time and life. But also it is about your family, your close friends and the people you care about.

What really count are the relationships we have—our family, friends, professional partners—the pleasurable encounters in our lives. We remember these positive moments, and they are all related to people we love and treasure. There is a genuine pleasure in meeting new people. These encounters are the highlight of the day, a ray of sunshine in the monotonous daily, business or social commitments.

There is the pleasure of being pleased, but also the pleasure of pleasing others. We all enjoy appreciation. Remember the nice feeling you have when you receive a genuine "thank you" after you have helped someone. The key phrases to use to express this relational pleasure are:

– "It's a great pleasure to see you Mr. Wang."
– "It's my pleasure to talk to you Mr. Wang."
– "I can tell you Mr. Wang that it's not every day I meet someone like you in my boutique. A real pleasure!"

3.3.6 Pleasure Of Intelligence

We all like to learn and enrich ourselves. There is a great pleasure in understanding. Remember what joy you feel when you visit a museum, and someone explains the different pieces of art. Without a guide, you will only see colors, shapes and drawings. When an expert tour guide explains the art to you, guides you, your visit is definitely a success. You only really appreciate what you are able to understand, not what you see.

With your affluent customers, engage their intelligence. Bring food for thought into the conversation, add value and make them understand the magical world of your brand. Tell the story of the house you are showing— all the happy events that have taken place in this house. And when a customer notices something about the house, compliment them. Your customer has made the effort to take a close look. We all enjoy appreciation. Therefore, why not bring the pleasure of sharing into the process. Experience has taught me that wealthy customers are on the whole outgoing people and always have a lot to tell you, to teach you. Sharing is a true joy.

You will be surprised by how curious customers can be, and how open to learning and appreciative they are. Be generous and share. Be appreciative and happy when customers share. Engage without the selling objective being the sole aim; be in the conversation for pleasure and you will be able to develop a genuine rapport.

3.3.7 Luxury Is About Pleasure

Pleasure should be at the center of the conversation. High-end valuable products carry the association of a gentle, caring, pleasing relationship. Different clients have different expectations when it comes to enjoyment and this is the privilege of being able to advise wealthy customers on high-end products.

During the conversation with Mrs. Michelle Taylor, pleasure could have been mentioned in various ways:

- *"What a pleasure to have you visiting today."*
- *"Please, how can I assist you?"*
- *"Assisting you is a real pleasure."*
- *"I am sure that your husband will be so pleased to find just the right gift for you."*
- *"I want to be able to help you find the perfect gift for your wife."*
- *"Madame, I am sure that it's a pleasure for your husband to buy this if you really like it."*

Luxury buying is a positive act. Luxury might not be necessary (in the functional sense of the word) but it is essential as an aspect of the human need for self-affirmation and also for the pleasure it provides. It is useful, it can be a social necessity and it is an economic reality.

And, why not?

3.4   New Clients: New Money, New Generation

It is obvious when you walk down Paris's Rue Saint-Honoré, London's Bond Street or New York's Fifth Avenue that the clientele is young, and many of them are Asian or international workers or visitors. We discuss the specifics of the international visitors in Section 3.5. But first, we identify what all customers in the Luxury and high-end market have in common.

3.4.1 Brands and Only Brands

There is a new clientele that only buys brands. We are aware of brands from an early age. We are surrounded by brands and most items we own have a brand (even fruit and vegetables are branded). This new clientele's journey with brands often started with their parents, who would prefer to give the best to their children, with the reassurance of branded merchandise. Later, as teenagers, brands forged a strong referential identity; along with musical preferences brands are part of an identity. In recent years, for many of us, brands have become symbols of a certain type of lifestyle.

New clients understand perfectly well the associations with Luxury brands. Moreover, many of them understand the strategy and the marketing behind the brands. They are not only impacted by the brands, they are also brand conscious and brand lovers. Brands represent an identity: I love this brand; you now know who I am. In Asia, many young clients do not hesitate to talk about Luxury fashion brands that they and friends like, both in conversations and on their social media pages; they form a part of their identity.

Our affluent clients wear brands, eat brands and use brands. For long-lasting goods, they will carefully select the brands they want to be part of their identity: cars, accessories and so on. With fashion brands, they want to be sure that they belong to the right group. Some even switch from one fashion brand to another, with a change in the designer, the new brand codes and colors. When they see their favorite "adopted" by people they don't recognize as themselves, they leave the brand—the group.

3.4.2 New Education

> ### Story Corner
>
> *When I was a little boy, I remember that my grandparents only wore blue, the workers' uniform of China. My parents had the chance to work for emerging companies in the new Chinese economy and I remember that my father wore only gray suits, or blue jackets with white shirts. The men of today's young generation like me are adopting branded styles rather than expressing their own personality. I only wear black suits. Luxury brands facilitate our choices. Of course, my children are different: they just look weird.*

The New World economy has been strongly impacted by the rise of China, and immense wealth has been created in other countries such as Korea, Brazil and India. With China, and territories such as Taiwan, Hong Kong and Macau forming Greater China, immense wealth has been generated during the last 25 years. This new clientele consumes Luxury creations with pleasure, discovering the quality, and learning how to appreciate and self-reward with the best from around the world.

Unlike in the Old World, where wealth, like the mindset of Luxury, is passed down from one generation to the next, in some regions there is an entirely new mindset emerging in Luxury consumption. Our new clients have no one in their history to emulate—customers have to acquire this cultural aspect by themselves. Wearing jewelry is a good example; when your parents do not wear jewelry, you are not used to wearing it either and you may not know how to match jewelry with attire. The same goes for make-up. Luxury advisors should make the most of this exceptional opportunity to fulfill this special need for advice—on products and beyond products—for their customers.

3.4.3 No Complex and No Guilt

Clients are sometimes brand customers before being able to afford Luxury brands. Many of them (especially in Asia) are used to Luxury, with wealthy parents buying Luxury products for themselves but also for their children. In Hong Kong or Japan, many of the Luxury fashion brands propose exclusive children's wear, with great success. These parents simply want to offer the same brand to their children as to themselves. These parents do not see their children having other handbags or watches other than branded ones, for reasons of quality and also the strong desire to give them the best possible in life.

Buying branded Luxury is a journey. When starting a working life, Luxury creations become part of the affirmation of self, the pleasures and the self-reward. In China, Japan and Korea, for example, the first of these luxury self-reward gifts is often a nice watch or a branded handbag and not necessarily a nice vacation. The product is aspirational, a way to access a certain category—it satisfies a social need.

For many wealthy clients, buying Luxury is just like selecting a nice restaurant to go to or a nice hotel to stay in. It is about having the best possible life, for themselves but also for their family and close friends. More than a specific lifestyle choice, for many of the very affluent it's simply a case of selecting the best in a category. Your customer is just shopping like everyone else.

3.4.4 Abundance Of Information

Internet and mobile access to information of course changes everything in the way consumers behave and in particular toward the high-end, high value products. Browsing online, looking for information and going to forums have become part of the purchasing journey—learning first, before purchasing, is becoming natural.

The abundance of information also creates uncertainty; consumers need to take more time to discover the truth. There are so many forums, self-acclaimed gurus and potential experts, but also smart liars and thieves. Even though you know how to find information, you never can be entirely sure that you really have the facts.

Your client needs good advice, now more than ever before, from reliable people who are genuinely there to help them.

3.4.5 Abundance Of Propositions

Luxury *maisons* have never been so powerful or so numerous. There are also new creative brands, emerging every day, in all categories. A brand can emerge in only a few years, while some have been established for over a century. Brands are launching sub-brands, such as seen in the motor trade, with each line becoming a brand in itself. And Luxury brands have also seriously increased the pace in collection changes and launches—with new offers and strong advertising campaigns aggressively saturating the market.

The life cycle of these Luxury products is also shorter. Just look at the considerable number of handbags offered in the market, along with the extraordinary choice for wristwatches.

There is also more and more impulse buying. Some affluent customers, after watching the news and talking with some friends, could simply decide to buy a *pied-à-terre* in the south of France, Portugal or Suzhou. Lisa wants the Italian fashion brand bag because it was the right product to have, at this time. She might, in a few weeks, switch her attention to another brand.

Sales advisors need to fully understand the brand and the product environment, to remain up to date in order to advise.

Golden Rule Corner

Be as informed as your clients.
If I know, you must know.

3.4.6 The Client In A Hurry

The pace of professional, and also private, life has increased extraordinarily with communication via the internet, mobile messaging and so on. Since every piece of information is available at all times, and anyone can access it, there is an overwhelming feeling of the need to know everything, professionally but also in one's private life. In addition, with traveling and time differences, our customers are always connected and "plugged in."

Expectations in terms of communication have also changed with mobile messaging. A letter used to be answered within one week. Email tends to be answered within one day. Mobile messages are expected to be answered immediately.

Most of the time, wealthy clients live in urban areas, if not in mega cities, where they benefit from extraordinary service. In Tokyo, Hong Kong and New York, online orders are delivered the same day. Wealthy customers expect the same level of performance from sales advisors.
They are impatient—be quick.

Golden Rule Corner

Be as informed as your clients.
If I know, you must know.

3.4.7 Clients' Expectations

Wealthy customers expect the same level of service and information as is advertised on the corporate website. They do not accept tomorrow for an answer when today is possible. They expect the best, and this includes the way information and service are delivered—fully and quickly. Traveling around the world is also part of wealthy customer's lifestyle. They expect a service at the level of their lifestyle and this applies wherever they are in the world: buying at the best price regardless of where they purchase and benefiting from the brand's sales advisors offering them the service they deserve—the best.

3.5 International Clientele

It is obviously difficult to classify customers into groups. It might even be counterproductive to do so. Therefore we explore here only the key characteristics to uncover the main things sales advisors need to pay attention to when Luxury selling to affluent customers worldwide.

3.5.1 Know Where Your Guests Are From

It's always very surprising to discover how little most people know about different countries. The world is becoming smaller and Luxury sales advisors have the privilege of the world coming to their doorstep. Being aware of key facts about different countries will make you feel closer to your customers, and naturally, you will be nicer and in tune with them. We always like things better when we are familiar with them

Be familiar with the geography, but also be curious. Each country has key facts to understand; take the time to enrich your horizons. It is not only useful but enjoyable. The world is your playground and you have a great chance to meet people of different nationalities.

You can engage in a small conversation with your guest from Taiwan or Libya; they will find your general knowledge refreshing. Prepare questions; show your interest. Your guests will be appreciative and will welcome telling you about their country.

3.5.2 Be Yourself, Be Natural

Being natural—yourself—whatever the type of client in front of you is the general guideline to be adopted, especially with international wealthy clientele. It doesn't prevent you from adapting, but never go beyond this. Avoid behaving too differently from how you would behave with clients generally. Thinking that you will be able to better serve your customer by copying their behavior is a very common mistake with international clientele.

The first danger to avoid is to think that you should adopt certain mannerisms because your client thinks in a certain way due to cultural differences. Most of the time, these anticipations are wrong. Customers, whatever their nationality, expect the same level of service, and look for the best sales advisor as discussed in Chapter 1. Globally, the best sales advisors act consistently and in the same manner regardless of their cultural background or the cultural background of their clients.

The second potential area of discomfort in the relationship can come about from you making it difficult for your customer to anticipate your behavior. When you try to behave like someone you are not, your clients will be puzzled or confused. Some might even find your behavior funny. But they will never see this as a plus, unless you are able to completely adapt the total social code and rules, and are perceived as totally bi-cultural.

Also set some limits; do not go beyond what is possible in a conversation. Sales advisors should avoid talking about politics and religion—even if invited to do so. For example, Chinese customers sometimes like to hear your opinion about China but be sure to not get into any political commentary. Never go down these alleys simply because you never know what your client really thinks and you are not there to make personal comments. There are many other potentially interesting and neutral subjects to discuss.

Story Corner

Naga-san, a senior executive in Japan told me that bowing is a very complicated affair. In some companies, there are full-day training sessions on bowing etiquette: to whom, when and how. There are even degrees of angle according to whom you are bowing. It's a sign of politeness and also very explicit in the relationship. How can I learn all this subtlety I asked him? Well, just don't bow, he said. As a foreigner, you do not bow in your country and therefore you don't need to bow when you meet customers in Japan. I insisted: I want to show my respect for the Japanese culture and can absolutely learn. Well, Naga-san told me, in doing so you create a problem for yourself and your customers. You can try to learn but you will always do it wrong. Your customers, upon seeing you bowing, will be surprised and might not know how to react. "What shall I do then," I asked. "Why don't you just shake their hands?" he said with big smile.

Of course, you can proceed the way you would usually: bowing, kissing and shaking hands. The most important thing is to really be yourself, not pretend or be fake, and not forcing anything. Sincerity is the relationship anchor.

3.5.3 Beware Of Physical Contact

One of the most sensitive issues is that of possible physical contact when selling Luxury creations that require assistance. In general, male sales advisor should avoid touching female clients.

A first simple recommendation is to always ask politely for permission before proceeding. Some experienced sales advisors tend to believe that creating possible physical contact with the customer helps to gain trust and makes sales easier. I tend to believe that physical contact can be off-putting and should only be reserved for clients with whom you have a long-standing relationship. Physical contact can take the form of a social act in many countries (shaking hands and so on) but mostly it remains in the private sphere if not in the exclusive family space. Or even only in the intimate one.

3.5.4 European Customers: Heritage and Emotion

Western Luxury clients, notably in France, the UK, Italy and Spain are often initiated into Luxury. They may have assimilated (maybe even the whole family has) part of the cultural heritage of brands. They enjoy high quality and know how to appreciate it. They are educated and look for the emotion that Luxury creations can bring them.

Some buy a small piece of that heritage, for a wedding or for an anniversary for example. It's a real educational choice, a tribute to the quality and the brand legacy. I cannot encourage enough that a sales advisor should take particular care of these clients even if they seem to be "small" clients. They are significantly more important than most sales advisors realize because these clients take immense care in their choice in quality.

In their decision making process, European clients look for stories and romance. They have more appetite for meaning, being able to go beyond the object. Of course, art and spiritual elevation are at the center of this, in their vision of what a qualitative world should be.

It is also a very frequently required exercise, when dealing with European customers, to be able to respond to their objections. While Asian customers do not object (they listen and choose whether to believe or not), European customers tend to ask questions in order to get answers. It's a way for them to explore the different possibilities, and sales advisors have to be prepared.

3.5.5 Russian and Middle Eastern Customers: Exceptions and Privileges

Russian customers admire the heritage of European Luxury brands. An elite customer traveling around the world has a strong appetite for the best, if not for the exceptional. Russian customers tend to adopt a strong attitude, and sometimes do not hesitate to "test" sales advisors. They are also known to be very fair, and can be loyal when sales advisors earn their trust.

3.5.6 Middle Eastern Customers: Exclusivity and Importance

Middle Eastern customers mainly buy abroad, and in the summertime—when they travel to avoid the heat in their own countries. Many Middle Eastern customers are highly educated, most having been to school in London or Switzerland. They often belong to very wealthy families. There are a few recommendations when dealing with customers from the Middle East: be discreet (never mention the names of other Middle Eastern clients you might have), be natural (shopping is part of their enjoyment in visiting Western countries, together with the freedom they can enjoy there).

With Middle Eastern customers, there are sometimes question about how to deal with women and the different religious dress codes. Many customers from the Middle East are dressed in the same way as Europeans. Just behave naturally. You do not even need to ask where they come from. They might want to enjoy that space and their dress code tells you to behave exactly as you would do with any other person in your boutique. When female customers are dressed in religious garments, a female sales advisor is necessary to sell or at least to assist. When they are not dressed religiously, just provide the same service that you would provide to all your clients.

3.5.7 Japanese Customers: Tradition and Perfection

Japanese clients are definitely the most educated Luxury clientele. They not only consume Luxury, they thoroughly learn about Luxury brands and are aware of why they choose one brand over another. When a Japanese client buys, he must know why he buys. They love the tradition of artisans in the creations. Generation after generation, artisans work patiently to achieve the best possible quality. It is an endless quest that Japanese customers want to be part of. Perfection is the ultimate goal and a Luxury creation product should be as close as possible to this ideal. The artisan working on the brand's offering is always trying to progress toward perfection.

Japanese clients are also fully informed when they visit. Some may even make an appointment in order to benefit from the best possible experience. There is no place for improvisation—for the client, or for the sales advisor receiving them into their boutique.

Story Corner

In Japan, a customer came to a Luxury car exhibition and was interested in a specific model. The sales advisor offered much advice. The client nodded, approving of the professionalism of the sales advisor. The service was good and the client agreed to leave his contact number. An appointment was made a few weeks later at the showroom. This time the customer visited with his wife. The young couple expressed their interest, notably about the different possible options and additional services—but they still needed to reconsider everything. A third meeting was organized and this time the young couple was there to listen to the sales advisor, who offered some additional options and services in order to obtain their positive decision. Payment facilitation was proposed; the young couple expressed their agreement and an appointment was made right away for the following week in order to sign the contract. At the fourth appointment, the contract was prepared and the director of the showroom came to thank the young couple personally on their choice. Another appointment was made for delivery of the car. I asked the sales advisor why it took so long, and why there were so many appointments. He answered simply that: "In Japan, customers are very professional."

3.5.8 American Customers

With American customers, your professionalism will be your success.
They really appreciate self-confident, knowledgeable and helpful sales advisors. My advice is to be proactive and fearless. They want to see happy, successful sales advisors.

Of course it's a pretty general first view. But it should allow you to avoid big mistakes. Be understanding and natural—just be a nice person.

3.6 Digital Impact

3.6.1 Digital Age

From printed media (newspapers and magazines) to aired (television and radio), information has become digital (TV, desktop computers, laptops, tablets, cellphones).

Reading habits have also changed. Information is expected "now":

– Everywhere (I can always be connected)
– Anytime (I can always have access when I want)
– In any way (I am free to access in the way I like)
– Unlimited (There is always the information I need, if I want it)
– Uncontrolled (I can have access to most information independently)
– Free (Effort is needed but most of the information is free)

This new freedom gives the feeling of POWER to the customer—and it is important to integrate this aspect of the Information Age in the selling process. A Luxury and wealthy customer is educated and connected. He knows that he can get all the information by himself, independently.

The counterpart to this new Digital Age for customers is that information is also:

- Time consuming (There is always a price—the time you need to find it)
- Unverified (Many scams and errors can take place online)
- Too dense (Very difficult to digest)
- Not memorized (Too much, too quick)
- Potentially dangerous (Manipulative)
- Mass (Not personalized)

Sales advisors facing this new information paradigm should remain confident in their role and continue to offer the best possible service to clients. Customers have access to digital information but they have no time for that. His or her time is more precious, and is devoted to the business and/or family.

Henry: "Mr. Hudson, I understand that you have studied our financial offer online before coming to see me. I hope it didn't take too much of your precious time. I am sure that I can explain to you better than the screen because you can tell me what you want and I can tailor the information to you. That's why my bank needs me, in order to provide you with personalized and only useful information, to simplify your decision."

3.6.2 The Need For Multimedia

The new Information Age is also one of images: photos, videos and audio. Customers tend to read less, preferring to look at videos and pictures. Information has to be entertaining and deserve attention.

In the selling process, when needed and appropriate, do not hesitate to add photos, videos and audio. Customers' attention is short. Instead of explaining to the new generation, show a video and let the images speak. Videos should be short, images easy to understand, and audio smooth and pleasant.

Customers are in the fully blended communication network every day. Adapt yourself: mix words, videos, pictures and audio. The multi-channel communication network allows the sales advisor to retain the attention of the client, and reinforce his messages by proving what is clearly true: the images.

3.6.3 The Conversational Mode

Customers do not want only to receive information; they also want to contribute. They want a conversation (social media) and do not want to be broadcasted to. They look for the social link rather than an institutional site. They tend to view the official establishment as suspicious. They reject manipulation.

Sales advisors need to adopt a particular attitude when facing customers who are used to the conversation mode. Instead of lecturing, sales advisors could try what is known as the upstream information technique.

Henry: "Mr Hudson, you know, what is marvelous about my job? It's that most of the time our clients have already spent time online and studied our financial offer. I therefore prefer to start by listening to you. Please, just tell me about what you understood and, ask me all the questions you have."

Moreover, customers hate to be told what they already know—what everyone already knows. Good information must be new information—and new information that counts for the customer is the *right* information. Customers look for exclusivity. Instead of retelling the brand story and always repeating the official statements, the products' features and so on, it is always useful instead to go online and study the history–the story–of the brand, to enchant and create romance.

Henry: "Mr. Hudson, on our corporate website, you probably have seen that we focus mainly on our history, being one of the most trustworthy financial institutions for over 250 years. It looks like any other private banking presentation. I proudly have spent 15 years in this bank and let me tell you, that from the inside, we understand what being trustworthy means. In my personal view, people working in this bank all know that without our clients' trust, we would all be out of a job. And if you have time, I can certainly tell you a few stories of the relationships we have built between clients and financial advisors."

3.6.4 Peer-To-Peer As Authoritative

Peer-to-peer information sharing is dramatically changing the way in which customers make decisions. Many blogs and collectors' sites are featuring luxury items, with reviews from owners. Similar to travel sites where visitors can comment and assess a hotel's details, customers simply follow the logic that:

— The person I can trust is the one who really did it, or is the one who owns it
— The person I can trust is the one who has no interest in lying
— The person I can trust is the one who is trusted by others

A second reasoning is, the person I can really trust is one similar to me: "This customer group I belong to cannot lie to me because they do not have any interest in influencing me."

For a purchase, a client will search for real experience feedback, a neutral opinion, and advice from a network. Consultation within a network is also a way to create links and strengthen connections with friends.

Sales advisors have to take into account this preference for trust, and use it as a real contribution in the selling process.

Henry: "Mr. Hudson, I am not sure if you also had time to check different blogs dedicated to private banking. There are a few, very well documented, and our bank and services receive significant recognition. Of course, if you wish, I can email you links to these websites."

3.6.5 The Cross-Border Phenomenon

With markets becoming transparent (easy to get product information and prices) and the possibility of sending almost anything at relatively low cost by international shipping and courier services, more and more consumers are buying across borders.

Local import duties, goods and services taxes, and operating costs generate pricing gaps and provide opportunities to a very large of number of professional buyers who prospect Luxury and high value products online. Sometimes, vendors are organized into large corporations, finding goods and selling on a very large scale, notably into the Chinese market, but not only.

Sales advisors have to know that these channels exist and they had better know and understand them. When facing a customer claiming to be able to find a Luxury creation he wants at a much lower price, it is important for the sales advisor to raise the arguments and state the risks of not buying from an official source:

– Fakes: Some operators will even fake certificates of authenticity and even the packaging and the shopping bag
– Pre-used: You never know if a product has used. Everything can be faked
– Degraded: Some internal parts can be changed/substituted for parts of a lower quality
– Modified: Some features are removed or changed into lower quality (for example, diamonds)

Lucy: "Mrs. Lam, I know that there are some sites proposing our iconic handbag at the price you mention. I am not sure if they are actually real. Even if they are real, they might be exchanged items or pre-used. You know, these days, some operators can fake anything including price tags and even shopping bags. Sometimes there are operators who don't even know that they are not selling the original item because they buy their goods from unreliable sources—from who knows where. Of course, the handbag could be original, just the same as this one, but there is a risk that it is not genuine. We do need to be vigilant, when it comes to buying online from strangers."

In the digital age, the role of sales advisor is changing drastically. The advisory role is there not only to provide information but to assist customers in the decision. Not only is there a need for true expertise, but sales advisors also have to be able to assist in the emotional and experiential aspect:

– Provide the right information to ME
– Reassure ME

3.7   Chinese Customers: Some Keys For Success

Chinese Luxury consumers account for 30%–40% of worldwide Luxury consumption, if not 50%, for some product categories. And Chinese customers do not only buy Luxury products but also invest in high-rise properties, cars, education programs and so on. And they buy worldwide—just walk down New York's Fifth Avenue or Paris's Rue Saint-Honoré. If you have a chance to be in Monaco, Nice, or Portofino, today the Chinese own the best properties and luxury cars. Even with a recent slowdown in Chinese Luxury consumption, China remains the second largest world economy and the nation is the number one consumer of Luxury products.

I observed that many of sales advisors—owing to a language barrier or cultural differences—are not comfortable serving Chinese customers. Some are even judgmental, and worse, disapproving. As a sales advisor, first and foremost, you need to respect Chinese consumers.

3.7.1 Sentiment and Appreciation

There is quite often resentment toward Chinese tourist consumers. Japanese tourists in Europe, years ago, were perceived as always carrying a camera. Today, Chinese tourists in Europe do not enjoy a good image.

Most of the time, they still travel in a group (though less and less) because it is easier, since a very large majority to not speak English (English language education was not part of their school curriculum). The younger generation will dare to travel independently; but most Chinese tourists prefer traveling in groups with friends or family. Always being "in a group" makes them more obvious somehow, highly visible. They are in a rush when they visit Western countries as there is so much to see. They dart from Milan to Paris, and to London. For many of them this is their first visit to Europe or to the USA. It is certainly stressful, especially because sometimes no one helps them, and they also have to constantly protect themselves from theft and touristic traps (they have heard many stories of such things before traveling).

Despite the language barrier, and their limited time frame, Chinese tourists have to combine sightseeing and shopping. They have little time to spend and many products to buy! Before arriving in Paris, they most likely have already prepared a list of what they will buy for themselves, but also for family and friends—basically to save money or to find items that are not yet released in China. We have to understand that they are tired of waiting in long queues outside some luxury stores, and once inside the store they do not speak or understand English, Italian or French. And they have to wait a long time to see the products that they already know they want to buy. Some sales advisors tend to complain about Chinese tourists and the fact that they buy Luxury without the Luxury codes. Many Chinese tourists visiting Europe feel disappointed about the service they receive: slow and unfriendly.

Should we show more appreciation? They are new consumers willing to share our passion for creativity and quality and therefore allow the industry of Luxury and high-end products to be able to continue to exist. The tremendous recent development of *haute horlogerie* is a good example, with more and more Chinese consumers knowing more and more about time-pieces. There is no art without admirers, and buyers.

Chinese consumers are also buying properties and financing expensive education programs for their children. They are creating jobs, financing economies and they do participate in the development of the Luxury industry, allowing the creation of many employment opportunities.

With a positive state of mind, and better appreciation, you can learn how to better handle Chinese tourist consumers.

3.7.2 Recognize Chinese Consumers

The different Chinese tourist customers can be easily identified. First one can separate the Chinese tourists living in China from the Chinese coming mainly from Taiwan, Hong Kong and Singapore.

Most of the time, Chinese from Hong Kong, Taiwan are Singapore do not travel in a group and do speak English. Sales advisors do not have too many difficulties with these customers and just have to deal with them as naturally as possible.

We want to focus more on Chinese visitors who deserve your special attention in particular. The first challenge for you is to distinguish a Chinese customer. Of course, it will be easier if you speak Chinese. Instead, why don't you start by watching Chinese movies in the original version so that you can discern the Chinese language? You can easily distinguish spoken Chinese from Japanese and Korean, for example. The second piece of advice is to obtain clues, for example, from the handbag of Madame or the wrist-watch of Monsieur. Most of the time, you will see a nicely branded handbag for a woman. For a man, there is a good chance that he will be wearing a nice branded bracelet timepiece. I tend to suggest not looking at their dress code in general. Do not be surprised to see men in very casual attire; business owners in China do not wear suits and comfortable attire is always preferred. Do not be surprised to see ladies in high heels, sometimes seemingly over-dressed for shopping or sightseeing. It is important for them to be well dressed at all times, to always look good in pictures but also to be able to match the beauty of the cities they visit.

3.7.3 Why Do Chinese Tourists Buy So Many Luxury Products?

Whenever you ask a Chinese person why the Chinese love to buy Luxury items, the answer is quite often the same. When you can afford Luxury, why would you not buy Luxury? I often hear that Chinese customers buy for reasons of "face" (social status) and for gifting. It is true and certainly these reasons play a role in their decision to buy. But contrary to some perceptions, Chinese customers buy simply because Luxury products are superior. They buy those items that are not produced in China. They do not buy brands without consideration; they have an idea of what the best brands are and are simply buying the best (from the top ten watch brands or the top five cosmetic brands and so on).

Acknowledge that Chinese consumers buy brands and Luxury products just like you and me. They simply expect the best quality and brands are an easy way to guarantee that they received that quality. They are ready to pay a high sum for something China does not have, for example a particular tradition of watch and jewelry design or leather goods—a certain art of living. They are also convinced that having the best is key and it is simply a part of the way of life of the social elite. This comes from a long tradition when the imperial and the social elite's main pleasure and occupation was to find the best to enjoy.

It is also necessary in China to show some success in order to gain social credibility. Gifting is also part of the hospitality culture; it is a way of expressing gratitude and is part of the social codes. Chinese consumers do not benefit from items and so on passed down through the generations or heritage. It is now that they are on their way to acquiring jewelry, watches and properties that they will be able to pass down to the next generation.

Chinese tourists also buy abroad because of tax reasons; their savings could reach 30% or more compared to local retail in China and you can understand that, with the tax savings on Luxury goods, they can quite literally cover the cost of their trip. They also buy for family and friends, and this is why they end up with such large shopping lists.

3.7.4 Dealing With Chinese Tourists

When they travel Chinese tourists are particularly impatient. It is true that they do have to optimize their shopping time. And shopping is definitely part of the program, and for many of them is even the main objective. Buying abroad offers a cost saving for them, and a guarantee that the products are genuine. Besides, they are buying in the country where the product has been made (which is even more meaningful). And for sure, Chinese tourists do come for the quality and service experience of a Luxury boutique.

I still believe that sales advisors do need to take the necessary time. A Chinese tourist will never reproach quality service. They only despise slow service, a lack of efficiency. Communicate, charm and provide the same service as you would to other clients and you will be surprised by the response.

Story Corner

Marie is a sales advisor at the flagship store of one of the world's leading leather goods brands. Every day she has to deal with impatient Chinese tourists. "Just give them what they ask for quickly," was the advice given by her colleagues. Marie decided to proceed differently. When she received a list of bags from the Chinese client, she used the three sentences she had learnt in Chinese:
"Thank you, I will get the creations right away."
Adding: "I will also introduce a few new creations."
"Please, take your time making your selection."

Marie always manages to up-sell, cross-sell and receives very positive customer feedback.

3.7.5 Selling To Chinese Customers

In a normal situation, what advice can be offered for selling to Chinese customers, taking into account the cultural differences? More and more Chinese customers do speak English.

You need to sell yourself first, before selling your products. The key is your capability to quickly establish confidence in you. And it's not really any more difficult to establish a relationship with a Chinese customer than with any other. It is about showing empathy, generosity and sincerity. Respect is important and might be one of the key differences.

Converse with and behave naturally is my second piece of advice. More and more Chinese customers do speak English. But you can learn a few Chinese sentences, like Marie did, to be able to communicate and show respect to your Chinese customers. But never pretend that you can speak a little Chinese, unless you are very proficient. Unfortunately, for most of us, it is easier and better to learn to speak English fluently. Always speak clearly and slowly enough to allow your customer to understand what you are saying.

> ### Golden Rule Corner
> Speak slowly and simply in English. More and more Chinese tourists understand English if you make an effort to make it easier.

Accept with intelligence cultural differences and other personal behavior. Your customer may seem rude when they speak, in a rustic way, or when they handle your Luxury creations. They may not understand the etiquette in Luxury goods. You may be surprised that they can behave in a certain way. This is a sentiment of superiority and one to absolutely avoid. Most of these customers are highly educated, with strong leadership positions. They are not impressed by Luxury— for many of these customers, the items are to be used in daily life.

Being extremely courteous is always necessary. You need to be aware of a few important rules. Firstly, never become too familiar. A client is a client even when he treats you like a friend. Never make the mistake of taking your client for a friend. If your client is a particularly friendly client, still make sure you avoid getting into conversations of a private nature unless your Chinese customer offers such information. Wait for him to tell you and if he does, be sure to remember what he told you. The second rule is to not be in too much of a hurry. Let things come naturally; time is the best facilitator.

Some sales advisors have the impression that it is difficult to know what the Chinese customer's decision is. It is pretty simple. Chinese customers never commit unless they are absolutely sure about their decision. If they are sure, they will tell you. And if they are not sure yet, they will never say yes and you have to keep selling. The same expectation applies to you: if you are not fully sure, don't commit.

I also hear that Chinese customers do not say no. Chinese customers do say no like everyone else and most sales advisors simply do not know how to detect the no. Some expressions that mean no are:

"It's okay, thank you."
"No need for the moment, thank you."
"That's all for the moment, thank you."
"I need to leave now, thank you."

When a customer has already said no, you can always try but you need to find another angle–another product or a different way to keep the conversation going.

Understanding what a Chinese customer is really telling you will come with more experience.

3.7.6 Build a Relationship With Your Chinese Customers

Despite the language barrier, it is always possible to build a long-term relationship with a Chinese customer. All you need is a WeChat account, they will easily exchange their contact details with you via your WeChat account. They are generally very happy to have foreign contacts and will even help to introduce new clients to you that may be visiting your city.

I also suggest you go the extra mile for your Chinese customers. In the Chinese culture, there is a great sense of gratitude and they will always reciprocate one way or another to thank you for the additional and personal service you provided.

3.8   Client Psychology

3.8.1 Luxury Selling Is About Psychology

Luxury selling is about selling Luxury creations to wealthy customers. It's also about selling high value products to any customer. The Luxury Selling method is based on a new approach of understanding the customer's psychology to sell any product to any customer when a true decision process is necessary.

Peter Wang acquires a few watches a year. He loves to take the necessary time to consider his purchase—it is a kind of chasing pleasure. Finding a rare pearl that some others may not be able to discern is his pride. He is patiently building his collection. His trigger point might be his pride in being one of the most prominent watch collectors in Asia.

Michelle Taylor needs to be sure she is making the right choice; it is a wedding anniversary gift from her husband and it cannot be the wrong choice. The couple need to make this choice memorable. It is an important memento for them and they came to Paris especially for it, and also to build this memory together. The trigger point might be the great experience at the boutique and they want to extend it with the purchasing decision.

John Hudson is not buying a Luxury car every year. It might be a great experience at the car showroom but you never know. Car sales advisors are usually very good and he had better be very careful. It is also a decision that impacts the family budget and Paul does feel bad that he will spend such a large amount on a car that he is driving. It is an important decision, emotionally, even if ultimately the monthly payment is not that high compared to his monthly revenue. Paul needs to feel good and relaxed with this new car—not to feel guilty—and have the impression that he made a great decision for himself but also for his family.

Lisa Lam is looking for a treat. The handbag she is seriously considering is from a brand that she has never bought before. She is attracted by the buzz around this new handbag but still not sure if she should follow her impulse or stick to her preferred brand. Her trigger point might not be the bag but the brand; she needs to adopt the brand as well as the bag.

Paul Morgan's intention is to optimize his personal finance with life insurance. He has always doubted these financial plans—preferring other, simpler and more transparent investments such as properties, stocks and bonds. He is feeling that this is something that he needs to reassess.

Sophie and Allan Williams have to make an important decision in buying their new home. It is certainly a very high price. More importantly, it might mean a good decision that they can be very proud of. Or it could be a bad decision and they will blame themselves. And they need to decide quickly— nice properties do not stay on the market for long.

The right approach is to ask yourself what the client's needs might be; it is advisable to keep this in mind and prompt yourself to understand the client's motivations. These are the real triggers.

Why are they here today?
Why today and not before?
Why are they using their precious time visiting you?
Why not something else?
Why have they chosen this brand?

3.8.2 Psychology Is About ME, and How Others See ME

Customers are all different—they do have different expectations. But, they always have one common point—what I call, "the ME."

How I see myself

How I want people to see me

Hans does not need to appear successful. He sees himself as very smart and intelligent. He is sensitive to ideas of "being able to master" something—for example, mastering time. By not buying expensive clothes he is telling others that he is above caring too much about his personal look and what his peers may think of him. It is possibly just another expression of telling others about they way he is—who he is. A good sales advisor would see that Hans' need to feel that he is making smart decisions is his trigger—for Hans it is that feeling of being different.

Brian Morgan visited a private bank without his wife. He might want to be able to take all the time he needs to understand the various options. This makes him feel like he is taking responsibility. If he comes with his wife, he might want to show her how much he cares about family protection. Maybe Brian has more to tell, and it is not only about signing a new investment. His care for his family is in the background and that is why he is here today— rather than simply studying the yield of the return on investment. A good sales advisor would deal with this part of the psychology. A lack of understanding of this may lead a sales advisor to only focus on the product, instead of the customer.

Instead of guessing who your customer is, ask yourself how your customer sees himself or herself? They own their perception of themselves and will tell you about their expectations and the way these expectations should be addressed.

How do they want other people to see them?

Instead of guessing who they are, it would be better to detect the external signs which show how your customer wants others to see them.

3.8.3 Ego Expression

There is nothing bad about ego as long as it is not harmful or disturbing. We all have and we all need a dose of ego. It all depends on how this ego is expressed. Customers love to talk about themselves. All you have to do is to open that space for them. Once customers are in the space, most of the time they really enjoy the experience and will reveal more and more. Talking is also a pleasure. Here are a few techniques to invite the customer to open up:

* ***Invite the customer to talk about his world***

It is particularly joyful to be able to tell people what we do—to talk about our life. Affluent customers are more willing to share than people usually expect. And most of the time they share simply, nicely and with a lot of humility.

Martial with Peter Wang:

- *"Mr. Wang, you must have traveled a lot. I really cannot imagine how hectic your life must be."*
- *"It's okay; after so many years I am really used to it."*
- *"May I ask where is your home or where you feel at home?"*
- *"That's a good question…and my wife also asked me. You know, I just told her that home is where she and my kids are."*
- *"That's very touching Mr. Wang."*

• *Invite the customer to talk about their peers*

Talking about peers might often be easier than talking about oneself. It is always meaningful for someone able to listen carefully. Customers reveal themselves by talking about others.

- *"Mr. Wang, as a collector, I am sure that you must also know many other collectors who share your passion."*
- *"There are many who claim to be collectors but believe me, they just buy and do not really collect."*
- *"What do you mean?"*
- *"They don't really know and sometimes are wrongly advised by sales staff."*
- *"You are certainly a discerning collector, that's why I really value your appreciation. And I will be very proud if you could take a decision on our creations."*

• *Invite your customer to share*

We all have a secret garden, some very exclusive information that we love to share—when asked. Sharing provides many joys because giving is a pleasing gesture.

- *"Mr. Wang, I am sure that you also follow many blogs? Are there any particular ones you would recommend to me?"*

• *Compliment your customer*

We all like compliments—especially when they are sincere and appropriate. Customers tend to respond to compliments and offer more information about themselves. It is sometimes a way for a customer to share their appreciation.

- *"I am so impressed about how much you already know about us. How come you don't just do like the others who only pay attention to the major brands?"*
- *"Actually, I started collecting watches before the recent fervor around watches erupted. I don't like buying the brands everyone else has. Many of the watches in my collection are from the time when no one knew about these brands. If I am wearing a brand that everyone is talking about, I find it very showy. I am definitely not the type of person to show off."*

- **Giving importance to your customer**

Pay full attention to your customer and you will be rewarded. A customer who feels important will talk easily, and confide in you.

– *"Mr. Wong, you are a very important person to our brand. We would like to know more about how you see our brand."*

- **Asking a favor from your customer**

Why not ask for a favor when it is appropriate? It creates a more personal relationship and also valorizes the customer. By asking a favor, you are also telling the customer that you believe in her/his generosity and you are offering a unique chance to prove it.

– *"Mr. Wang, could you help me understand more about high-level collectors? Are there any clubs in your country?"*

The more you are able to get your customer to talk about themselves, the more you will understand not only his psychological mindset, but also his ego.

Golden Rule Corner

Speak to the customer's ego – unveil the customer's mindset.

We all care about our own ego. Ego is the reason for why we want to look good, to be admired and to make the effort to succeed. It is part of our own identity and there is nothing bad about that. Ego gives us energy, drive and the eagerness to seeking a better life.

3.8.4 Influence Positively

Your company, your brand and your products are great; nevertheless, customers always have other choices. Sometimes the offers from your competition are not better. Moreover, most of the time, products are not really comparable anyway. What is the best jewelry for Mrs. Michelle Taylor, if not the one that the couple had decided upon together? What is the best financial plan for Paul Morgan if not the one which can give him the satisfaction of having protected his family in the best way he believes he can? There are certainly many rational facts in these choices but there are also many psychological factors.

Whatever you are selling, be it a Luxury creation, a car, a property or a financial investment, you are not only selling a product to a person. You are talking to the ego of that person. You are a person influencing another person. For that, you need to be a person with a soul in order to be able to reach the essence of the person in front of you.

We will see in the following chapter how this influence can be exercised, notably by understanding what persuasion is, and how customers take decisions following five motivational factors.

Luxury selling is about being able to understand your customer's psychology and finding ways to influence effectively. It is never about money. The high price makes evaluation necessary, but never makes the purchase impossible.

As I explained in Chapter 1, a sales advisor needs to be someone the customer can trust. A customer will only unveil themselves to someone he/she can trust. In Chapter 2, I walked you through the various possible customer mindsets.

We will consider in Chapter 4, the buying motivation and the decision process.

4

Luxury Selling

4.1 Active Selling

I started talking about Luxury selling by inviting sales advisors to adopt a real Luxury attitude. In the second chapter, we mainly walked through the customer's psychology. Now you are ready to understand what Luxury selling is, meaning a successful encounter between a sales advisor and a customer. Let us start to ask ourselves what the reasons are for buying, and what might be the causes of unsuccessful sales.

Thinking Corner

For products/services you are selling—why do customers somtimes not buy? What are the most frequent situations encountered?

4.1.1 Reasons For Buying: Desire

The classic economic model is copied and pasted into a selling pattern, but in an incorrect way. For many, a sales person ought to know the need (request) of the client in order to be able to propose the right product (offer). The demand and supply theory might be true in economic sciences but it is not fully applicable when selling to valued clients.

First difference: the offer sometimes generates the demand. For Luxury items, there is no real demand. Why would you need another handbag

© The Author(s) 2017
F. Srun, *Luxury Selling*, DOI 10.1007/978-3-319-45525-9_4

when you don't even know how many handbags you already own? Buying Luxury can be done on impulse. It is not only because there is demand that a sales advisor can sell. Of course, the Marketing Department is usually responsible for creating demand. However, in a boutique environment, a good sales advisor can sometimes successfully generate the desire for a new handbag in a customer who came into the shop for something else.

The idea of desire is also very complex when talking about end consumers. In the case of B-to-B buyers, one would establish a book of specifications, define the budget, the timing and the purchase strategy. Usually, end consumers do not take the time to clarify their need. From the point of view of the sales advisor it is an impulse buy. This is not only because it is very often, not clearly expressed. Customers might want to have something as a self-reward. It could be a handbag, but which one? Which brand? What about the design? And even budget is more about a price range, an idea of the sort of money you need for a great handbag. Finally, the timing is not defined and customers hope to find the right product with an opportunistic approach.

Instead of focusing on requests, let us speak about desire. Desire is what drives a customer to enter the boutique, to spend time looking for new products. Desire is complex but at the same time opens many potential selling opportunities. It might be desire for a certain brand: a customer could buy different creations from the same brand. If the desire is primarily to fulfill the need for a self-reward, it could then be something significant for pleasure.

Lisa has no real request other than a vague desire to have a new handbag. Even to her, the desire probably remains unclear. She just has a feeling that she wants to treat herself to a new bag. Or, is this desire due to the adverts for a specific handbag that she keeps seeing in magazines?

When Lisa saw that handbag, she just loved it! "It is so hip, and very trendy," she said to herself. She liked the color, the shape, the interior lining. It is desirable and she feels she would very much like to have it. The brand—from the Creation Department, to Production and of course Marketing—has done a great job. The sales advisor made a brilliant final step by providing a great presentation. That original vague desire is becoming much more real and an experienced sales advisor knows, above all, how to establish a bridge between customer and product. An effective sales advisor is also a creator of emotions, and acts as part of the entire emotional charge of the Luxury product that he/she is selling.

4.1.2 Reasons For Not Buying: Fear

But Lisa might not want to buy it immediately. Maybe this is because it is from a new Italian brand with which she is not familiar. Also, the handbag could be a little bit small, in her opinion. Or the price: since she has never purchased this new brand before, she is not very sure about such an expense. The sales advisor is very good, for sure, but since this is the first time she has met her, she is not able to gain the full trust of the customer. Last but not least, Lisa might tell herself to not rush: buying a handbag is not urgent and she might think she should take more time to look over other things on offer. She will then give the classic and terrifying (for a sales advisor) comment "let me think about it."

When customers do not buy, of course you are disappointed. But few sales advisors actually ask themselves why the customer did not go ahead with a purchase. What were the reasons that the customer did not buy? There is only one important factor that blocks the purchase decision: fear.

The customer is taking an important decision—not just in terms of the purchase value but due to the fact that someone like Lisa simply does not buy a branded handbag every day, every week or every month—and customers feel that there is a risk of getting it wrong. Therefore, the safest thing for a customer is to postpone the decision. This is again not a decision about the money involved but rather to avoid making a mistake. When the fear is stronger than the desire, a customer always follows their basic instinct: to escape from the danger.

In the case of B-to-B, professional buyers would establish a list of criteria for the decision. And since a decision needs to be taken, the buyer can compare the different options, rate them and choose the best one. The final decision might be rated as only fulfilling 80% of the criteria, but since it was deemed to be the best option, it still makes it the optimal choice.

For the end customer, a "yes" has to be a fully convincing one. The decision not only has to be the best decision, but also a happy decision. A customer never buys with only 80% satisfaction, and never buys with potential regrets. Purchasing Luxury is all about purchasing pleasure.

We will see in the following chapters how you can increase the customer's desire to purchase, but more importantly, the different ways to reduce the fear of purchasing—notably by dealing with objections elegantly (Chart 4.1).

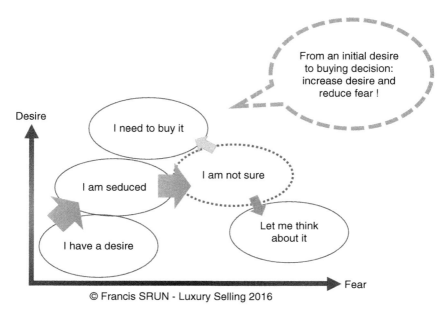

From an initial desire to buying decision: increase desire and reduce fear !

Desire

I need to buy it

I am not sure

I am seduced

Let me think about it

I have a desire

Fear

© Francis SRUN - Luxury Selling 2016

Chart 4.1 Between desire and fear

Golden Rule Corner

Focus on desire but do not forget the fear.
Fear is powerful and the main reason for not buying.

4.1.3 Rationale For Decision Making

The rational part of the decision process is related mainly the functional part of the product. For Lisa, her bag has to be a certain size, a certain weight, a specific color, a certain type of leather. Even when it seems rational, it is not precise. Lisa does not want a bag that is too big but cannot tell us exactly what she means by "too big". The sales advisor must figure out what size she really wants.

Customers are not always aware of the different rational criteria involved in taking a decision. What appears to be rational most of the time can end up more or less confused and simply result in "I like it" or "I don't like it" responses. Customers also very often express their rational criteria in an emotional way. It is in the listening, discovery phase that the sales advisor should be able to clarify what the rationale is—and attempt to elucidate what customers really want in those terms.

Lucy: "How about this new creation, also from the spring collection?"

Lisa: "No, I don't like it…"

Lucy: "Is it because of the size, color or design?"

Lisa: "No, it's too big and yes, the color is too dark."

Lucy: "I understand. Size is very important! Let me show you the smaller version that we have. Let me also introduce a few other colors—there are some very attractive options in our new collection."

4.1.4 Emotion In The Decision Making Process

A major part of the decision relies on emotional factors. Lisa is not only looking for the right size, a nice color and a designer handbag. She needs something new to feel good about, she wants something that she desires and she just feels like buying another handbag.

The first emotion is created by the brand. The same handbag, with a different brand's logo on it will appear differently to your customer. This brand's image is in your customer's mindset and it is worth exploiting it to the maximum level. We will extensively speak about it soon, brand being one of the most important motivation factors in buying.

Let's get back to Paul Morgan and Roger with the decision on subscribing to a financial savings plan:

Paul: "Well, I understand that long-term investment is necessary in any case, but 20 years is really very long."

Roger: "Mr. Morgan, we are, as you know, not just a bank. We are an institution that has existed for over 150 years and we have even been servicing many families for multiple generations."

Paul: "Will that will mean that I am locked-in and obliged to pay premiums for 20 years?"

Roger: "This will be a thing of pride, sir, to start a plan and to be able to keep it going for your family. You are creating a tradition that will make your wife and children proud!"

Even if understanding the rational factors is important in order to be able to advise wisely, what really makes customers take a decision is often the emotional factors. Emotional factors satisfy their true desires.

To convince Lisa to go for the handbag, Lucy could focus on the emotional factors rather than the functional ones:

Lisa:	"The colors you have are not really the ones I am looking for."
Lucy:	"I understand that you are imagining a certain color. How about looking at these nuances, carefully chosen by our Creative Director? If you don't have a very precise idea of color in mind, how would you feel about considering these very bright colors?"
Lisa:	"Sure, they are nice colors."
Lucy:	"That's why I invite you to consider and take more time to feel the beauty of this Sangria Red, Midnight Blue and Fruity Yellow."

Golden Rule Corner

A decision is rational and emotional.
Talk to the mind and to the heart!

4.1.5 Tension and Stress

Since it is an important purchase financially speaking, but also on the emotional side, customers do have real tension throughout the decision making process. You need to be aware of this psychological load and be a true partner to customers.

Sophie and Thomas Williams are with Simon, their property agent:

Thomas:	"I know it's our 2nd visit but we are not sure we are ready."
Sophie:	"It's much bigger than what we wanted at first."
Simon:	"Do you mean that it's too big?"
Sophie:	"It's never too big...I'm just not sure if we need so many rooms!"
Simon:	"As your advisor, may I help by telling you that this might not be the main reason you are not ready for taking the decision."
Thomas:	"I think he is right Sophie, it's just we are not ready for such a big house but we don't mind, right?"

Simon: "A big house involves more housework. Will you both be involved in caring for the house?"

Simon: "You are right Sophie, I did not think about this aspect and a big house will definitely need more daily housework. And Thomas is probably thinking first about the comfort of you and kids, and being able to have more space to live in!"

Sophie: "I don't know, there is just so much to think about."

Simon: "It's a very positive sign, Sophie, that you are already projecting what it would be like living in this house. My agency has also partners such as a home helpers agency and home maintenance centers—it's very convenient in Singapore and you will find more assistance than you could imagine."

Customer tension depends on the main criteria:

– The amount (monetary importance)
– The frequency (habit of making such a purchase)

These tensions appear and increase when it is close to decision time. There will be objections and even apparent rejection. It is about finding a way to calm the fear, sometimes negatively (Chart 4.2).

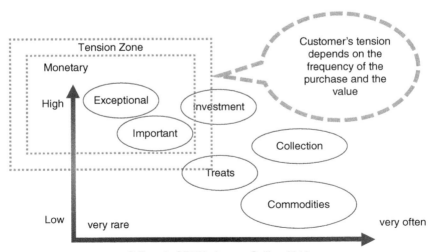

© Francis SRUN - Luxury Selling 2016

Chart 4.2   Customer tension

4.2   Persuasion

In the previous section, we realized that a customer's decision making process is subject to desires rather than needs: the more a customer desires something, the more willing he is to commit. But, at the same time, a customer can have fears. And fears are reasons for unsuccessful sales. To succeed, the sales advisor will need to generate strong desires and reduce all fears. Sales advisors will need to manage the emotional part of the decision, not just the rational aspect.

To achieve good results, it is important to know that the true spirit of Luxury selling is persuasion. I believe that this is one of the most important elements of this book. I invite you to fully understand the power of the persuasive approach.

Story Corner

A kingdom was attacked and the king asked his ministers and his son to advise. The general said: "My Lord, we have to strike back now, we will win, I am sure. We need to keep our kingdom." The prime minister said: "No my Lord, we cannot win the battle for sure. We have to negotiate our surrender. At least then we don't have to sacrifice so many people."
The king asked the prince what they should do.
"My Lord, you know that I am in favor of striking back. But I have to tell you that I am not sure if we will win the battle. But there is also chance that we will. On the surrendering option, I am sure that we will lose our kingdom. The decision is yours, my Lord."

4.2.1   Convincing A Customer?

At school and at work, we need to prove that what we say is right. At work, we have to convince colleagues and defend a project. It could be called making a case. A common example would be that of a lawyer bringing proof to their arguments. Another would be the hero who convinces everyone by being very inspired himself. Another type of superhero could be a politician, full of conviction and able to get everyone to endorse his beliefs and affirm his leadership. In many cases, self-confidence is the key and it is about talking loudly, with conviction and showing self-confidence.

When you try to convince someone of something, you are stating your views and confronting their ideas. You are telling each other your positions and everyone is supposed to explain their views. You will succeed if you are able to convince the others. Success is achieved when your proposition is adopted and you manage to have everyone recognize that your's is the best solution. This is a pretty routine exercise in professional life.

It does not work the same way in Luxury selling. By trying to convince your customer with your arguments, you want to demonstrate that you are right, which therefore means that your customer has to be wrong. And if you manage to get your customer to take a decision, it means that you succeeded in imposing your view.

Let us keep looking at Paul. An inexperienced sales advisor tries to get him to sign up to a 20-year investment plan with a convincing approach:

Paul: "I still don't see the point of subscribing for 20 years."
Advisor: "Okay, it's really what is the best for you in terms of return on investment."
Paul: "Why not only 10 years or 15? And how could you be certain about the return on investment with such an unstable economy?"
Advisor: "Well, just let me show you why you should subscribe for 20 years and not less, Mr. Morgan. You will see and you will understand why you should subscribe for 20 years. A longer period is really the best for you."
Paul: "Well, you can always try but I warn you, I am very hard to convince."

The word convince comes from Latin, meaning to conquer or vanquish. It implies the notion of battling, opposition. By telling him that subscribing for 20 years is the best option, the inexperienced sales advisor will attempt to demonstrate that he is right. Paul is not receptive: why would give his attention only to be told that he is wrong? There is inevitable tension. There is a winner and someone has to compromise and accept, be a loser in the confrontation.

You can easily see that there is danger in this sort of approach to convincing a customer. Your customer is not an opponent, and he wants to be right. Even if he accepts your proposal, you need your customer to be happy and not left feeling like the loser in the conversation. More than anything, you want your customer to be happy, very happy about the decision he is taking. How can he be happy if he feels that he has had to change his initial state of mind? How can he be happy if he feels that he has no choice but to accept the sales advisor's position? Even if he understands that the advisor is right, it is still not pleasant to be wrong.

4.2.1.1   Using The Persuasive Approach

Roger, young but talented, is using a different approach:

Paul: "I still don't see the point in subscribing for 20 years."

Roger: "I understand—20 years is quite a long time! The decision will be yours, and you absolutely could invest for a shorter time. As your advisor, I do not clearly see the benefits of a shorter investment time, but would love to double-check with you. Why don't we go over the options again and you tell me which one you feel is better for you."

Paul: "Sure, walk me through the different options and let's see together which one is best for me."

Roger: "I am now changing the investment period on the simulation tables. How about trying 10, 15 and also 25-five years to compare with the 20 years we mentioned initially? Just to have a look."

Paul: "Don't tell me you are trying to up-sell me to a longer time-scale of 25 years?"

Roger: "Oh no Mr. Morgan. It's just to give you the full picture. Many of our clients go for 20, 25 and even longer. It really depends on the personal objectives and situation. No harm in checking, right? And that's what I am here for, to help you to make the best decision."

Paul: "Okay, show me the differences please."

Given this example, are you able to spot the differences in terms of approaching the same situation?

Table 4.2.A Differences in convincing and persuasive approach

Convincing Approach	Persuasive Approach
You should take this decision!	The right decision belongs to you!
This is the best option	Do you see a better decision than this one?
You cannot be wrong by taking this decision	You know that you are taking the right decision.
You should decide now, not wait	You can decide any time, but why would you wait?

The first courtesy is to recognize that your customer is not an opponent, but a client. And as a client, he can tell you anything and freely give his view. Your client will always feel that he is right—never show a client that he is wrong: this is a key general rule of business. The 2nd and most important consideration is that your customer knows better than you do, what is very good for him. This is simply because he is the one who will take the final decision (Table 4.2.A).

These two acceptances are key in the persuasive approach:

– Your customer is always right, even you think or feel differently
– Your customer knows better than you do, what is right for him

Because your customer is always the one who will make the final decision, as a sales advisor you can only influence the decision making process.

To achieve this, the sales advisor must adopt a more neutral position, rather than focus solely on the sale: advisors, consultants, ambassadors, personal finance experts all need to be able to adopt the neutral position. This will generate a sentiment of partnership in your customer. It also means a non-conflict position. Instead of giving arguments, the sales advisor will provide information, studies, proposals, options and possibilities. Instead of pushing to the decision, the approach is to have the customer agree to further examine the proposal together.

Let us go back to Lisa and her handbag (Table 4.2.B).

Persuasion is about accepting that the decision comes only from your customer. And your customer will take a decision more easily if they are convinced, by their own thinking, that they are taking the right decision. In using the persuasive approach, you need to give the reins to the customer. The customer is the center of your focus, and must never be seen as an opponent.

Table 4.2.B Different approaches, handbag example

Convincing Approach	Persuasive Approach
The handbag is a very good size—just right—not too big or too small!	You have many, many handbags I am sure and you know better than I do that this handbag is just the right size for every-day use.
The color is very trendy, I am sure you will like it	I believe that this color goes very well with the design—don't you think so?
It is a very nice design and is high qual-ity. It is not expensive at all!	A handbag that reaches this level of quality is necessarily at this price, or even much higher, and you might even know this better than I do!
You can trust me, it is a very good buy and you look very nice with this handbag	Why don't you trust yourself? It is a very good buy and you look very nice with this handbag. Just look yourself in the mirror!

4.2.2 In Transactional Mode

At school and at work we are asked to be affirmative and self-confident. But one also has to remember that living with others and working on group projects requires teamwork. It is about being able to understand others' positions, moving from one's own position to a position that is the best for everyone. Being able to do these things are also the signs of a true leader. An efficient Manager can convince and can make decisions but is also able to compromise.

Golden Rule Corner

Always look for a potential agreement.

4.2.3 Harmless Manipulation

To manipulate is to influence someone to act in a certain way that is detrimental to the interests of that person.

As a sales advisor, you certainly want to lead customers to take decisions in a way which is favorable to you. In the persuasive approach, there is certainly the objective of influencing the customer to take a decision. But the decision is not necessarily harmful to the customer. If they do not buy from your brand, they might buy from another brand anyway. Even if you persuade the customer to buy, as far as the act of purchasing is concerned, it is something that will not likely put the financial situation of your customer in danger. You are only making a new and happy customer.

Sales advisor:	"Mr. Hudson, how do you rate the different options?"
John:	"Well, it's true that the shorter savings plan definitely provides less protection and therefore I have less interest in subscribing to it."
Sales advisor:	"Indeed, it's an important decision and you were absolutely right to raise this point. Shall we, for the moment, stay on the 20-year assumption, and look together at the different investment instruments within your plan?"

Persuade, rather than convince. Be soft and fluid in the way you sell. Throughout this chapter, we will keep on demonstrating the power of the persuasive approach—along with the selling process.

4.3   The Five Motivational Factors

4.3.1 Specific Decision Process

When you visit a supermarket weekly, there are only a few decisions to be made. And if there are any, the decisions should be quick and simple. But if you want to buy a pair of elegant shoes, you will probably want to take more time over the purchasing process. Price is evidently the first factor. But there are many other factors too.

You will be confronted by many choices. Will you go back to your favorite brand or try a new shoemaker? Should you try and get a lower price, or upgrade this time to a higher price level product? What could be the budget range or maximum? Will you go back to your usual boutique or shopping areas to research your purchase or even wait for a trip abroad? Will you buy now or in few months as your shoes are still in satisfying condition at the moment?

There is always a decision making process involved when you are making an exceptional purchase. This exceptional situation might be due to the high value of the product (something you cannot afford all the time), the long duration of its potential use (something you don't need to buy all

Table 4.3.A Products status

	High Value	Very High Value	Exceptional Budget
Personal	Shoes	Watches	Sports car
Exceptional	Luxury getaway weekend with wife	Custom-made shoes	Secondary residence
Emotional	Wedding rings	Wedding anniversary gift	Art pieces
Long-lasting	Desktop computer	Family car	House

the time) or because of the high emotional impact (something you really care about).

The products could be at different levels of price.

Let us have a look at a few examples, for Mr. Wong and his lifestyle (Table 4.3.A):

4.3.2 The Five Decisional Factors

Let us imagine you want to buy a new car. What would your decision criteria be? Do you want an estate car, an SUV? What about exciting options (GPS, leather seats, etc.)? But more than that: you most certainly have an idea of the brand you want, a brand that you really trust or that you aspire to own. You have an idea of the budget that you are willing to devote to it, that will match the expectations of your wife or husband. You also worry where you should buy the car. For a new car, you have the choice between going to the official showroom or a dealer (who might be offering a better deal). For a pre-owned car, you would need to think what is best: to buy from an independent seller (would it be safe?) or from a car dealer. Last but not least, you would set a time frame. If this coincides with a family event (birth of a new child, moving or the like) then the time is more or less defined. Otherwise, you have more time and can take the time you need.

Let us look at John Hudson, looking for a new car (Table 4.3.B):

The five motivational decision making factors: brand, product, price, place and time correspond to functional, rational reasons. They are also deeply emotional factors, linked to feelings and sentiments. "It is about me and how I feel about these decisional factors." (Table 4.3.C).

Table 4.3.B Functional versus emotional need

	Functional Need	Emotional Need
Brand	My favorite make of car	I am fully satisfied with the German brand I have and am willing to purchase a new car from this brand. I am not thinking about any other brand.
Product	A 5-seater family car	I need a nice new car, a real upgrade compared to my current one. I need a comfortable car, a family vehicle but one suitable for other things too.
Price	Around $30,000	I am willing to spend this amount of money to give comfort to my family and to enhance my social status.
Place	Branded car showroom	For this new car, I will visit the brand showroom, in order to be sure to see the full choice of models but also the options, the service and after sales service.
Timing	This summer	With my new promotion to the position of Director, I would like to get this new car for summer time, and be able to go on summer vacation in it.

These factors are present in many different sorts of sales scenarios, and even apply to a financial investment plan decision—as in the one for Paul Morgan (Table 4.3.D):

With each client, I suggest you always structure the customer's exploratory path with a discovery plan. It will help you to be efficient, thereby saving your energy and allowing you to have a clear mindset, especially during the selling process.

4.3.3 Focus On The Key Factors First

Now that you agree on the existence of these 5 decisional factors, which one appears to be the most important? How would you rank them in terms of importance in the decision making process?

Table 4.3.C Motivational factors

Decision	Factors	Motivation	Questions Customers Ask
Why	Brand	Aspiration	Does this brand inspire me?
What	Product	Need	Does this product suit me?
How much	Price	Value	Does the price sounds like good value for me?
Where	Place	Services	Do the place and the people provide me with good service?
When	Time	Urgency	Do I want the product now?

Table 4.3.D Understanding real motivation

Decision	Factors	Motivation	Real Motivation
Why	Brand	Aspiration	I am looking for a very safe financial institution. This one has much credibility due to its serious image; the company's values speak to me.
What	Product	Need	I am looking for a savings plan for the worst-case scenario. I want my family, and especially my daughters, to be able to be secure until they have finished their college education.
How much	Price	Value	I am looking for a fair financial institution that will not abuse me with excessive charges. I am ready to invest the needed amount without compromising my lifestyle.
Where	Place	Services	I will only subscribe to a serious and renowned solid institution. I will not take any risks with my money. I will research the offer further with the Wealth Manager who seemed to be knowledgeable at our first meeting.
When	Time	Urgency	I think now is the right moment, that we have enough for opening a policy and feel the necessity to save more for rainy days when we are old.

Product, brand or price first? And what about timing?

For sure, the product is important. But it is not the only factor. Would John Hudson buy that sports car without the logo and what if the same car were not produced by a country as trustworthy as Germany but by an Asian country instead? Even if the quality is the same, the brand makes the difference. With the selection of a brand, the customer has already somehow pre-selected a certain set of values: quality, security, seriousness of a certain type of vehicle and at a certain price level.

Customers make decisions in light of these 5 factors and in this order:

Brand: The brand for me
Product: The product I want
Price: The price I should pay for it
Place: The place, the service I want to use it for
Time: The time I need it

The customer's need will be unveiled step-by-step, with motivation becoming more and more complex, but it will also become increasingly clear for you (Chart 4.3).

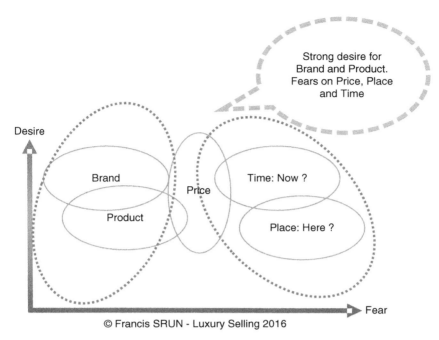

Chart 4.3   The five decisional factors

Let us recap:

A customer's decision making process is a balancing act between desire and fear. It always looks complex at first but by putting this method into practice, you will find it becomes increasingly transparent. Always keep in mind the five decision factors from the customers point of view: brand, product, price, place and time.

In the coming chapters, we are going to see the characteristics of each decisional factor and how to use these factors in a positive way to influence your affluent customers.

Thinking Corner

For the products or services you are selling, why do customers sometimes not buy? Brand? Product? Service? Price? Location? Time?

4.4   The Power Of The Brand

I briefly mentioned the importance of a brand name as a decision making factor. It is now time to go into detail about the power of brands.

4.4.1 Understand Your Brand

Just try and find a product that you use that does not come from a brand. Try hard—there is almost nothing on the market today without a brand. Even the less obvious items all have brands behind them. For example, when you buy fruit, vegetables and groceries you are also buying from a retailer, who is a brand, and gives you all the reassurance about the quality and price of your purchases.

It is key to understand how brands can help you influence your customer. A brand speaks to a customer often and very positively. Your best selling partner can be the asset of a brand.

• A brand is a person

A brand often has a name based on the founder of the brand. It is therefore more than just a logo—It is a man or woman with an ideal. The founder is perceived as an amazing person to have been able to achieve this. There are certainly a great number of reasons to explain why he or she was able to succeed. There will also have been some great moments, and maybe also some difficulties. There are always so many stories to tell.

• A brand is a creation

A brand is full of creativity: there is no success without innovation. Mentioning to your customer the key inventions will reinforce the brand's power. It is all about creation, invention and resilience. Your brand's creator could not have succeeded without being audacious and bringing something new. Very often, a brand creator is motivated by wanting to make this world better and he does so.

• A brand is a successful story

A brand is always a successful story. We all love success stories, and your brand, I am very sure, has successes to celebrate. Work on a 1-minute speech: how to tell to your brand's story like a fairy tale?

Let us have another look at Henry, advising John Hudson in the search for a new car:

Henry:	"You are already a happy owner of one of our cars and you can be very proud. Did you know that half a century ago we had already engineered the 4-wheel drive powering system?"
John:	"Oh, I did not know that. I thought that 4-wheel drive power was quite new."
Henry:	"That's why I allow myself to share our pride with you. Your new car will benefit from our long tradition of excellence, security, speed and control, as symbolized by the 4-wheel drive system."

• A brand is made of values

A brand is a made of strong values. These values are part of the DNA of a brand, and as such are transmitted and diffused throughout the organization. Why not share these values with your clients? If you do so, very often you will see joy from your customer, who also shares exactly the same values as your brand and its founder. They will feel they are part of your brand's tradition.

Henry:	"I know that all car makers are of course security focused. With our brand, and this since the founding of the company, security is not only an objective, it's an obsession."
John:	"What do you mean by obsession?"
Henry:	"In working for this brand for more than 15 years, I have learned that providing the safest car to our car owners is the number one priority. While some car makers will design fast cars, maybe faster ones than ours, we are always looking for the best balance between speed and safety. We always favor security over speed because you and your family's life cannot be compromised."

• A brand is a new territory

A brand has a territory to defend, and to expand. What is your brand's public image? What do customers know about your brand? What is already known by a customer can easily be exploited during the selling process. Maybe some potential customers have a bad or not a good enough idea about your brand. Excellent sales advisors should anticipate this and have very convincing messages ready in order to change any negative customer perceptions.

* A brand is full of symbols and emotions

A brand is full of symbols, representation and images. A brand takes time to build recognition for these things. Customers are very sensitive to what they can easily imagine.

> *Manager's Corner*
>
> *Engage your team to gain a better understanding of your brand with the method of storytelling. Each team member shall write his version of the brand's story. It is the story you would tell to your close family or best friends.*

4.4.2 Open The Brand Door

As seen previously, a customer's decision cannot be made without a certain band resonance. Your brand must speak to your customers. Why not to start to talk about your brand first? A customer who knows your brand will be able to learn new facts and consolidate a preference for your brand. A new customer to your brand will be delighted to learn and start the brand journey.

This is how Martial talks Peter Wong through his brand:

Martial: "I am sure that as a collector, you already know many things about our brand's founder, François Parly."

Peter: "Please, tell me more! It's still a new brand to me."

Martial: "First, François is a very nice person. When I met with him the first time, I was intimidated since, in Switzerland, he is considered to be one of the master watchmakers. He gently told us his story and why he decided to found his own brand."

Peter: "I was wondering about that as well—why some watchmakers manage to create new brands and why others just don't?"

Martial: "Parly told us that he decided to start his own venture in the middle of the night. He felt that what he imagined and would be able to offer would definitely be part of the history of watchmaking. He felt that it was his humble duty to keep on building up the more than 250-year tradition of fine watchmaking. I think that says it all. And it explains why this brand is what it is, today."

4.4.3 Be A Brand Ambassador

Being a brand ambassador is to intelligently exploit the brand's assets. Sales advisors have to be highly brand-compatible in order to become an ambassador for their brand. Adopt as quickly as possible the brand's look. This is the best way to express all your pride in your brand, but also to create immediate trust with your clients. Using the brand's vocabulary, but keeping it intelligible for your clients, along with the right attitude, will reinforce this trust (as seen in Chapter 1).

An ambassador is not only there to represent. A country's ambassador is also meant to defend the interests of the country. The role of the sales advisor is thus to defend the credentials of the brand every day, and keep on expanding the brand's territory by conquering new clients. Clients have choices and this role is not always an easy one.

Let's see how Lucy brings Lisa to her brand:

Lisa: "I have to say that your brand is new to me."

Lucy: "And we are very proud to have you visiting us! I am also very sure that my brand deserves your attention, and hopefully also your full satisfaction."

Lisa: "Are your leather goods all made in Italy?"

Lucy: "All our leather goods—all of them—are made in Italy. Unlike some other brands, and I don't want to mention names, we do not sell leather goods made in Asia. We insist on 'made in Italy' and made in-house, with all our expertise that has been built up over 3 generations."

Lisa: "Are some Italian branded products made in Asia?"

Lucy: "Yes, and I shall not comment on this. Please carefully check if your preferred brand does keep this integrity. We are definitely doing so, with pride, and for the full satisfaction of our clients."

In such cases, clients have to admit: "Yes, the sales advisor does really like working for this brand." Clients also expect the sales advisor to be proud and defend (with art and diplomacy of course) his own brand.

4.4.4 Insist On The Brand's Key Assets

A bank is also a brand—as Roger explained to Paul Morgan:

Paul: "I need to take more time and maybe consult my other bank."

Roger: "Mr. Morgan, I understand that the choice of the financial institution is key. We have been, for over half century, truly the leader in servicing families who want to build up their financial stability, and in providing necessary protection for their wealth. I believe that time will prove that we have nothing better to tell you, other than we are one of the most trustworthy organizations in the life insurance business."

Once you know what the key brand assets are, you need to tell customers, repeat them and insist on them. This is what is going to make the difference in the end. For Paul, what is crucial is not the financial charges—which are very difficult to calculate—nor is it about the yield over the next 20 years—which will be more speculative than rational. Rather, it is definitely all about the trust, the sentiment that "this is the bank I need."

Never take it for granted that your customer knows the assets of the brand. The benefits of evoking a brand are that, after you mention it, your customer will tell you how much he or she knows. And if there are any doubts, it will be an opportunity to deal with them. If you manage to defend your brand and convert your customer, you are halfway to finalizing a successful sale.

Paul: "Many institutions look the same to me."

Roger: "It is true and I really think that customers like you can discern true heritage from the marketing-speak. Our bank was founded in 1875, and has continuously serviced private clients like you. To us, you are not only a client but you are part of our tradition, our reason for being."

4.5   Product Desires

As seen previously, the brand is powerful and definitely influences the customer's decision in their purchase—very often unconsciously. But a customer does not think by way of decision making factors. A customer has first in mind the product or service he/she wants to acquire. The product or service is only one of the five decisional motivations, as seen previously. This is only the what, and not the why.

It is, however, the most evident one and understanding what a product really means is essential in order to present, seduce and influence a customer.

Most of the current writings about selling focus on need. We invite you to go beyond the need and the product so as to be able to influence more efficiently.

4.5.1 From Need To Desire

Simple products and services that we would like to purchase usually answer a need. When it is about high value products/services, most of the time they go beyond simple need. Need is basic but desire is something more complex, with different aspirations, and is much more difficult to discern.

We can take the example of the car John Hudson is looking for (Table 4.5.A):

Customers often express their needs by functional, factual matters. A professional sales advisor with experience and discernment is capable of translating

Table 4.5.A Expressed need versus real desire

Description/Item	Need	Desire
Brand: premium from Germany	A premium brand to fulfill the need for status	I like people to see me positively, like this brand I am driving.
Car size: 7-seater	More space for my family and guests	I like people to see that I have a large family, am in large group.
Car's power	A powerful engine	I like to have a powerful engine because I like to feel secure.
4-wheel drive power	Better control and driving comfort	I like to benefit from the sporty image of the brand.
Leather seats	Very warm and comfortable seating	I like luxury and want to feel at home when I drive.
Low petrol consumption	Reasonable spending	I like my family to see me as financially responsible.

from the expressed need to the possible desire. We will soon see the different techniques for discovering true desire.

Instead of focusing on need (often expressed by your customer) experienced sales advisors know how to approach the possible desire.

Paul: "We are a family of four but I am still considering a 7-seater car."

Henry: "Sure! Good idea! This model is not only a 7-seater but all the seats are very comfortable. Your children will be more than comfy at the back. And your guests will feel how generous you are by having such comfortable seats for them as well. It's as if you are inviting someone into your home."

Paul: "I also prefer 4-wheel drive steering. It's more comfortable and secure."

Henry: "Yes, you are young and active and definitely should go for the more sporty option."

4.5.2 From Functional To Emotional

Always ask yourself what does this product mean to your customer? Paul Morgan wants to subscribe to a life insurance policy. Is it only a financial investment gesture to get a high yield and make the best deal by doing a financial arbitrage?

Roger: "Mr. Morgan—might I know why you haven't thought about subscribing to life insurance before?"

Paul: "Well, I know that it's never a very good investment. You pay a lot and once something happens you get nothing. This is the underlying truth about insurance, right?"

Roger: "And might I ask you why life insurance is more important to you now?"

Paul: "Well, I feel that my wife would be more reassured if we had a policy. I also like to think that if something happened to me, at least the next 10 years of my daughter's educational fees will be covered, regardless our others assets and expenses."

Roger: "Mr. Hudson, you are such a responsible person. You are a loving husband and father and we'll make sure that we don't disappoint you."

Paul is highly motivated by showing love to his family. His investment is not only rational. You need of course to understand what is on his mind, to understand your customer. More importantly, you should try to open your own mindset to the customer's heart. If you are able to understand—often it might be just a feeling—what the emotional stakes are for your client, you will be closer to the desire and therefore the decision.

Golden Rule

The brain is rational and studies options.
The heart is vibrant and takes decisions.

The language and terms should therefore be emotional rather than just functional (Table 4.5.B):

Table 4.5.B Functional need versus emotional motivation

Functional	Emotional
Brand: Premium from Germany	"We are a brand that you can trust and be proud of! Our values resonate with you, I am sure. We have always been seen as the most reliable car manufacturer. First of all you want a car to be reliable, right?"
Car size: 7-seater	"This is indeed a generous car for your whole family and more. It is such a good feeling when you need to be able to have proper seats for your guests."
Car power	"This is a powerful vehicle. Our customers recognize that driving a powerful car gives more self-confidence because you always have that extra power when you need it. It gives real peace of mind!"
4-wheel drive power	"This car will give giving you incredible driving pleasure with a feeling of maximum control of the vehicle. It means that you always have that extra control power—you drive knowing that everything is there to assist you."
Leather seats	"Each time you take a seat in this car, you will feel the warmth, sense the softness and robustness of the leather and appreciate the pleasant natural fragrance of the leather. I am sure that it is a sensation that you cannot be without after you have experienced it."
Low petrol consumption	"This car gives the best value between security and spending. You do not need to have any strange feelings—it is incredible efficient for such a powerful engine."

4.5.3 From Product To Creation

A first suggestion: avoid using the word "product." It lacks exclusivity and evokes something that is produced in mass, by machines. If possible, choose different words when talking about your products.

A watch is a timepiece, a wristwatch, a timekeeper, an *horlogerie* creation. For jewelry, it is simply a jewelry creation or a precious creation. A life insurance policy is part of a lifetime financial plan, a long-term investment solution or a family savings package. A property your customer buys to live in is simply a family home. And, if he invests in a property, it is a property asset. The car that John will buy for his family is a family vehicle. By giving it a nicer name, we are also ascribing a different role to the product.

> **Golden Rule**
>
> Qualify the product differently so as to give more value and create emotional impact.

4.5.4 The Dimensions Of A Product

We can easily distinguish the two dimensions of a product: functional and cultural (Chart 4.4).

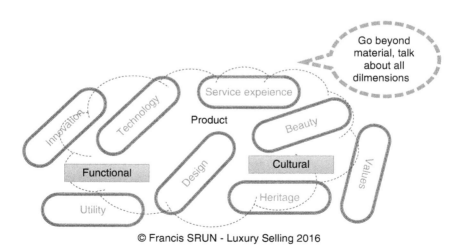

© Francis SRUN - Luxury Selling 2016

Chart 4.4   The dimensions of a product

- Functional

This is not only about the utility, let us also mention the innovation, the technology necessary behind each creation. The design is part of the functionality and is very often the most difficult part—the added value.

There is no great functionality achieved without proper research, serious work and innovation. Most first-class products have behind them leadership in involving *savoir-faire* and invention.

- Cultural

A high-end product necessarily has a strong cultural background. First, there is its heritage: the founder, the family, people who were at the origin of the success. The creation also carries many values, beliefs that make the creation different from other products. What are they? The creation is very often presented with a real retail and experience. Last but not least, there is a constant search for beauty in Luxury and high-end products.

The cultural dimension gives to the creation its real, rare personality.
A product is industrial whist a creation is unique. Your client is looking for something unique and exceptional. We will soon see how to present a product: how to romance and create the desire to purchase. Meanwhile, let me share with you a story about wine, as an invitation to always see beyond product.

Story Corner

I had the chance to live for 3 years in Bordeaux, studying at the Bordeaux Business School. I visited some of the most prestigious estates. But my most memorable experience was with a very small wine property owner in Médoc. After warmly welcoming us, the owner Louis walked our group of students to the grapes. While walking, he was talking about his family being there for only 60 years and how proud they are to take care of the vineyards. "We are still learning," he said, "about how we could deserve to be here, and our incredible luck to be winemakers." When he approached the grapes, he caressed the leaves, and invited us to touch and smell the grapes. He was also incredibly knowledgeable about geology and explained why the soil where we were is different from the soil of the property next door to his. "And also, the weather, a slight change in the soil's composition, the way we work on the grapes each year creates a diversity in grapes. You cannot really

> control Mother Earth." He walked us to the wine distillery, where we could see these huge stainless steel containers. There was also a small laboratory. Everything was so clean and neat. "There is no magic recipe to make great wine. We are only a sorcerer's apprentice and each time we have to respect was is given by Mother Earth, and handle it with care.". He finally took us to the barrels where the wines would rest and mature in oak wood. "We are always very stressed by how our wine will evolve in these barrels. Things are not always controllable; even if we do our very best." At this point of the visit I could not resist asking Louis: "Why are there so many uncertainties and therefore it looks like things are quite out of control. How can you be sure that you are going to be able to produce the best wine?"
>
> "They are creations, not products," Louis replied. "We are only making efforts every day to get the best quality grapes by protecting and nourishing our land. We handle with care what has been delivered to us, and we try with our experience to assemble what we can to get the best essence. After all, it's not in our control. We have to accept that!" Of course, at the end of our visit, Louis opened a bottle for us to taste and invited us to give him our comments. The wine was just divine. I will never look at that wine the same way again.

Go beyond product and the need. Understand the desire and then reinforce it.

Treat a product as a creation, by focusing on the emotion rather than the basic function.

Find all the dimensions for the products you are selling.

4.6 Price—Value

4.6.1 Price Level Perception

Sometimes prices for Luxury creations and high-end products might be intimidating to customers.

> *Story Corner*
>
> Mr. Wu is a very successful businessman from Taiwan. He happens also to be a very important collector of Chinese ceramics. Here is his story: "When I was a student, I always admired antique Chinese porcelain. I remember that my first purchase, made with my modest salary of an engineer, was a small white cup. It was nearly 3 months of my salary and it was, indeed, quite a crazy purchase! I started my own business and things went very well. A few years ago, I decided to devote 5% of my company's profit to my private collection. Today, frankly speaking, I just buy any piece I really want. The price? As long as it is in line

> with the fair market value, I can afford it. I have stopped thinking about my fortune and, by the way, I don't really know how much money I have. I miss the time and decision making excitement when I needed to think about each purchase and consider it compared to my yearly salary!"

A high-priced item, might seem high for a sales advisor, and probably is for many of us. Yet it might not seem high for someone who is living in a world that is used to that level of price. Your customer is probably not intimidated by the price. You do not need to worry about this point.

A price level is also related to the customer's wealth and capacity to finance it. For most of us, there is no such issue when we need to buy a pair of sneakers. We would focus on the brand, the model, the color and newness of what we are looking at. Unfortunately, for many very low income or no income persons, it is still the price that matters. It is the same with affluent customers. Even if the price looks high to you, it might be a relatively low price for your customer. It all depends on the base for comparison. For Mr. Wu, who does not know the exact amount of his fortune, the price is just a number and what really counts for him is what he gets in exchange for that number. He basically knows that the price is still reasonable compared to his total assets and he will not have problem in spending to purchase the item he wants.

Therefore, sales advisors have to place themselves at the level of their customers and see prices from another angle. The most important factor is not the price level but the fundamental question: is it worth buying? Customers always have the money for the product they seek to purchase. Otherwise, they would not be looking at it!

4.6.2 A Price Is A Value

Affluent customers live in a world of exchanging and trading money for goods and services. They probably trade more frequently than many others, especially successful businessmen. Some of them trade seriously high amounts; they are in an investment mindset every day. They buy stocks and companies. They chase rare art pieces. They always buy wisely, getting value for money and returns on their investments.

Their key question is never about whether the price they will have to pay is too high or not. If they consider it too high, it means they cannot afford it and therefore, would switch to another product, at a lower price. Their only concern when they can afford it is: is it worth it or not?

The decision on price is not only related to monetary value: your customer understands that quality products cannot be cheap. Price is not an issue, as long as it is:

– Affordable (the price is within his personal financial range)
– Fair (the perceived value is seen to be correct)

Most of the time, a customer is capable of buying anything they look at seriously. You always need to consider that your customer can afford it: if not now, maybe later. If not himself or herself, maybe someone else can purchase for them later.

There is very often doubt about the fairness of the price, especially that some brands and vendors targeting affluent customers do not hesitate in exaggerating and over-pricing products, so as to create desirability and to be able to offer discount prices in trying to get maximum profit. Affluent customers learn to be cautious: you have to be aware of these sorts of schemes when you are rich.

A price is perceived as fair, if it is true and sincere. And a price is seen as correct if the item is worth buying.

– A true price

In many places, it is still the case that the prices displayed are not the real ones. In some countries, you know that you have to ask for a discount, or wait for the promotion period. Some brands place full prices at a very high level, and then sell with price promotions giving 20%–50% discount. At property agencies in some countries the price displayed is subject to negotiation, with a large range of flexibility. Knowing that the prices displayed are not always true, the customer is cautious and doubtful. It is never easy to be sure that the price given is the real price. Customers need to feel reassured, and feel that they are given a true price.

– A sincere price

Some prices are high and one just does not understand why. The quality and added value are not there. Products might be over-priced and therefore the price is not sincere. The price, even if it is high, will be seen as correct if it reflects the quality of the product, the prestige of the brand and the exceptional quality of the service rendered. Price has to be seen as reasonable.

– A price has to be worth its value

A customer needs to see that the price reflects the product's value. Customers will compare similar products, brandsand categories. The price has to make sense and be justifiable. This is obviously the most difficult aspect to justify in order to convince customers to purchase.

Lisa:	"Your bag is not cheap!"
Lucy:	"It's because you have very good taste!"
Lisa:	"Is it under promotion?"
Lucy:	"Our leather creations are fairly priced, for the level of quality."
Lucy:	"It looks expensive for its size…"
Lucy:	"You might find a bigger bag for a lower price in a different brand, with a different design and probably a different quality of leather and level of craftsmanship. I can reassure you that you do not need to worry about the price value of our bag: it's fair and really worth it."

> **Golden Rule Corner**
>
> It is never about how much money something costs but it is about the value: how good is the product?

4.6.3 A Value Is An Addition of Values

A price can look high if you do not relate to what it represents. A nice leather handbag could be crafted with:

– Over 100 years of heritage in leather goods creation
– Leather selected carefully, regardless of the cost of the material
– Only the best part of the leather being selected, and therefore the more costly
– Hand-executed cutting and all processes done manually and individually
– Precise stitching, with over 20 hours of work for each handbag
– Double quality control processing for each handbag

Table 4.6.A Product value

	Cost For The Company	Value For The Customer	Expression Of The Added Value
Brand	Cost to build the positive image and maintain it	Brand image where the customer can benefit by acquiring the product	"We are one of the most reputed leather goods *maisons*" "We have true style, very distinguished."
Product	Cost to manufacture the product at the best possible quality level	Quality of the product	"It's not only a handbag, it's iconic." "The exceptional quality means you have nothing to worry about—it's just perfect." "You know, a high-quality handbag is not only beautiful but also crafted for long-term enjoyment."
Place, Service	Cost to build the boutique, and provide the excellent service	Pleasure of the surroundings; excellence of the service	"You can call me any time, my name is Patricia." "You will be invited to all our future events." "I hope you are satisfied with my service today and be sure that I will always do my best for you in the future."

Think about everything that costs money to your brand in the making of the product, and change the costs into value: there is a chance to give the added value to your customer, including the service provided. It might seem obvious, but it is still necessary to explain this to your customer (Table 4.6.A).

4.6.4 Defending Your Price

Sometimes customers do not question the price of your product, even if they do not understand why it is so high, and are thinking:

- The price is high because of the Marketing
- It is because there are always customers ready to buy
- Because it is a niche product and "the happy few" have to pay more

– General costs are too high in Europe
– That is how brands can make money

Customers tend to think that price is not related to reality, and even that it is arbitrarily set. It is up to the sales advisor to explain the reality of what the price tag means.

In order to do this effectively, sales advisors first have to be convinced themselves about the price of the product.

Quality costs money and there is no free lunch. A price is not a Marketing game but reflects a level of quality and sophistication. It is an expression of the brand's expectations but also customers' expectations. High-end and affluent customers do not look for a low-priced product but they do look for the best possible quality. They know how to appreciate the added value if it is well explained.

HOW TO: DO NOT FORGET COMPETITION

Managers tend to talk a lot about their own brand, with pride of course. They say why their brand is the best and why their prices are unbeatable. But they forget that competitors are doing the same thing. Customers do hear from other brands. There are different, very efficient and cost effective ways to increase competitive knowledge. Get all the printed products catalogs from the competition, including subscribing to their newsletters; get online catalogs too. And do market visits, surveying the competition to see novelties, and learn with your own eyes, which are just like your customer's eyes.

The more added value a sales advisor is able to communicate to a customer, the less chance that the customer will challenge the price.
We will more specifically talk about objection when we study the different price objections. The best way to prevent price objections is to defend the price before any possible objection is put forward by the customer.

4.6.5 Money Is Never An Issue

John: "It's not an easy decision, even if I really like it."
Henry: "Very happy to hear that you really like it. It is very important to me."
John: "But, I might not be rich enough to afford it."

Henry: "You know that not only can you afford it, you and your family deserve it! It's a great choice and you will really enjoy it, you will be very proud.
           Let's look at the different financing options we have for you."
John: "Even with a monthly payment scheme, it's quite a big amount."
Henry: "You know that it depends how to look at it."
John: "It's first about daily security, for you, your family and everyone you care about."
Henry: "It's also about durability and your peace of mind. A high-quality car can provide this for you.
           These are values that you really care about, so precious that money cannot buy, right?"

Money is never a problem. Your customers have it. It is matter of willingness to buy your brand, your product, at the price you propose, from you and right away.

The price level is never an issue as long as the sales advisor is comfortable in understanding costs and explaining the value to his customers. A Luxury creation, given that high value products are always carefully crafted, therefore need a sales advisor to explain them. A price is not a number made up by Marketing and does have solid reality behind it.

The price itself is a value, but also can represent many values. Customers are willing to buy high value products, simply because this is part of their search for quality. For these affluent customers, price is value: quality, authenticity, durability, security, positivity, strong personality—these values "that money can't buy" are precious and are offered by top brands.

4.7   Place—Service

We have seen in previous chapters the importance of brand, product and price in the purchasing decision making process. Since it is an important decision, and not always urgent, a customer will also consider where to buy and from who. We group this under the motivation called place.

This is where the magic happens: the place (Chart 4.5).

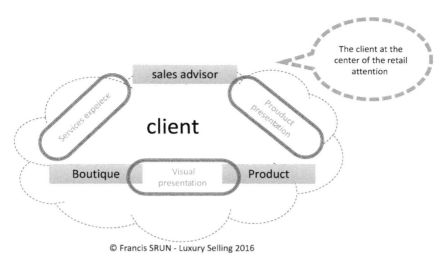

© Francis SRUN - Luxury Selling 2016

Chart 4.5   Retail: the right place for seduction

4.7.1 Customers Still Need A Retail Space

In the age of the internet and e-commerce, why do we still need a boutique, a place to meet? We actually probably don't need to go to a retail store, but want a better experience. The information is now available online. Paul Mason does not need to go to his car dealer's showroom to know about the latest launch, the new models, the options and prices, the available colors. He can easily pre-select and see all this information online. He could and probably did already check online articles from automobile magazines and blogs, and also the different comments from users and other car lovers.

A place is still relevant today, and I believe it will be tomorrow; it is something necessary for comfortably taking a final purchase decision. Paul, in spite of the 3D presentation offered by the car manufacturer's website, cannot get a complete sense of the real dimensions. He needs to sit in the car, to be able to fully appreciate the space and the comfort. He needs to drive it. He needs to check and double-check before making his final decision.

Customers' needs are different when they visit you. Some prefer to get information from the store, not being comfortable online (not familiar with using online portals). Others are fully prepared and informed, having done their initial research online, and come with questions and doubts and want to get confirmation and answers.

Taking the example of buying a car: Paul might have gone through different stages in his decision making process. Since this was an important decision, he might have been to the car showroom four times before finally making his decision (Table 4.7.A):

Lisa was browsing in the Luxury shopping mall on a Friday afternoon. She left the office an hour early and wanted to give herself the pleasure of browsing in small shops. When she decided to enter the Italian leather goods store, it was definitely just to have a look, especially at that handbag she had seen.

Lucy:	"Good afternoon Madame."
Lisa:	"Good afternoon."
Lucy:	"Welcome to B...the store is yours and I will be very pleased to assist you anytime."
Lucy:	"Thank you." (Lisa was pleased—she hates "sticky" sales associates.)

Table 4.7.A Attitude to adopt per stage

Objective	Customer	Sales Advisor
Initial Interest	Customer has a need and starts to look, without a clear idea yet. The need and desire is there but not clearly identified.	SA has to understand the need, even help the customer to better understand their own need. Less focus on product presentation but behave more like a knowledgeable friend.
First Search	Customer starts to browse. He is able to give a few ideas he has in mind. Still not really clear about a specific brand, product type or precise budget.	SA has to help in presenting the market, showing which brands and products are available. There is no worry that the customer would prefer another brand; this is the customer's choice anyway. The objective is to have the brand in the customer's preferred short-list.
Product Selection	Customer has few products in mind and is now comparing. Customer is now aware of brand, product type, budget. Timing is still flexible.	SA is there to further present and convince about the product and close the sale as soon as possible. It is always possible to close when the customer already has a selected product in mind.
Final Decision	Customer is now sure of the product and only comes to confirm their choice. Time frame is set.	SA has to reassure, confirm and congratulate the customer on their choice. There are still a few doubts but they are more concerned with after sales service, return policy and so forth. SA has to close in a very nice way.

Lucy:	"Madame, you are definitely looking at the most iconic choice of the moment. Please let me present our handbag to you."
Lisa:	"Don't worry, I'll just browse first."
Lucy:	"Sure Madame. I will prepare two handbags of different sizes for you to take a look at. You are so well dressed and so elegant—I really would love to have your comments!"
Lisa:	"Thank you! So this is the handbag in the magazines, right?"
Lucy:	"Absolutely."

Before paying for their purchase with their credit card, customers vote first with their feet. A customer coming into a retail space is never merely "just looking" or "just browsing." There is already a level of intention. Some desire must be there, whether it is clear or not.

Manager's Corner

In the multi-channel distribution environment, list with the team why customers will buy at your store or come to your office instead of going through other channels, including online.

4.7.2 Customers Still Need A Good Sales Advisor

A Luxury fashion label in London started offering an online service, part of the very trendy omni-channel strategy. The brand found out rapidly that there was a new business opportunity and was very satisfied with the decision of going online. One client in particular was quite intriguing: the client became the number one online client but they had a delivery address just five minutes' walk from the flagship store. One day, that client stopped buying. The Online Manager, having never contacted that client, wondered why and was not able to find any explanation. The Online Manager went to the flagship store and inquired whether the client had switched from online to the traditional store. "Oh no, answered the Retail Boutique Manager. Andrew just came in recently to tell us that he will move to New York and therefore cannot come to the store any more to browse, to have coffee with us." "Why wasn't he buying from store?" asked the Online Manager. "Andrew likes to try, to see, and not have the pressure of buying from us. He just wants to enjoy the personal shopper experience. Once he is at home, he makes his own choice, from among the different items he has selected, from our brand but also from others."

The role of sales advisor has changed. It has become something with a real advisory function. A good sales advisor can still make the difference. A customer wants to buy from a boutique, but more importantly from a person they can trust in that boutique.

John: "I also heard that different car dealers can give varying dis-counts to clients."

Henry: "We certainly will give you the best deal we can and I would be surprised if other showrooms will give you more off."

John: "I enjoy talking to you but want to be sure that my decision is right, buying here from you."

Henry: "Buying a car is an important decision because you are going to live several years with your beautiful new acquisition. If you need anything to better understand the car or if any further services are needed, you know that you can count on me. You just need to ring me and I can even take my car and come to see you."

4.7.3 Customers Have More and More Choices Of Places To Buy

Customers today have a great deal of choice in terms of where and how they make purchases. It is of course not always possible to use every available channel for any purchase (for example to buy a car from abroad) but customers today travel and their choices are much wider (Table 4.7.B).

Table 4.7.B Buy local or abroad

	Benefits	Risks/Disadvantage
Buy Locally	Convenience: no need to plan. Security: if anything goes wrong, can go back to see the sales advisor. Language facility: direct and easy communication. Possible for VIP treatment from the brand.	Prices: cost too expensive compared to abroad. Offer: not enough selection, not the latest models.
Buy Abroad	Prices: especially favorable in the country of origin. Customers travel as a couple and can make decisions together. Customers have time to enjoy the experience and shopping is part of the pleasure of traveling.	Security: need to travel home with the product. Lack of potential future services. Language gap: not always easy, nor a pleasure to deal with.

4.7.4 How To Make Customers Buy Locally and From You?

Lisa: "I will travel to Europe very soon, I can get it there."

Lucy: "Oh, yes! When do you travel and to where? Would you like me to help to check if this handbag is available there?"

Lisa: "Oh, I might have a business trip to Milan soon." (Not really true—Lisa is going to Moscow.)

Lucy: "You don't want to be disappointed. It could be just sold out and you will have missed it. In term of price differences, even if Duty Free, it's not really less expensive since we don't have GST in Hong Kong and therefore we can price more fairly compared to Europe."

Lucy: "You will need to go through the whole Duty Free process, claim and deal with airport uncertainties. Of course, if you wish I can calculate what might be the saving with Duty Free in Italy. Our experience tells us that that it's not always worth the effort.

Besides, you don't need extra stress during your business trip. Your time is very precious. And you can be sure that you will be part of our brand community and I will personally invite you to all the coming events.

My name is Lucy and I will be sure to always give you the best and most personal service there is!"

The only reason a customer would select another place or person to buy from would be to do with the quality and level of service and also possibly if there is a significant difference in price. Therefore, the sales advisor needs to make an effort to have customers decide on buying here (locally) and not there (abroad or from another retailer), in a secure place, without any possible loss and with the best possible service right now and in the future. It is about building a long-term relationship, knowing that customers always care about the service they receive—sometimes much more so than sales advisors tend to believe.

4.8   Five Times

We have seen in the previous chapter that one of the reasons for missing sales is that customers think they might have better options in buying abroad or through other channels.

4.8.1 "Now" Is Always Possible

Time is an important motivational and decision making factor, or should I say, the main reason for missing a sale. Customers often give this sharp and tough sentence to close their visit: "Let me think about it." Hearing this is terrible! Most of the time, when customers walk out the store, they do not really think about it, unless the buying/selling process has gone very well and only a few factors are still missing.

Let's face it—if the brand is the right one, the product the right choice, and the service is good, and since customers always have the money, why would your customer postpone the purchase?

Let's look at the timing factor in John Hudson's purchase (Table 4.8.A):

Customers use the time factor to delay their decision or to escape. It is always an expression of a certain doubt. And the doubt will generate fear. The fear

Table 4.8.A Customer time frame

Time Situation	Customer	Pro-active Sales Advisor
Real Time Frame	I will need the car only for summer time, in July, so it's not that urgent.	It's great and I fully respect your agenda! Let's book your family vehicle right now and should you want it earlier, we can of course still get it for you, Mr. Mason.
Vague Time Frame	I don't really need the car now, so I can wait.	It's great that you have taken your decision on this model and I am happy for you. Let's book it, and say for delivery within 3 months—does that sound right to you Mr. Mason?
Gaining Time	I need more time to consider. Let's say we take the decision next month.	I understand that it's always good to take more time in considering an important decision. What I am not really clear about is what is making you hesitate now, and how can I assist you in providing more facts to ease your decision on this wonderful model?
Escape	Let me think about it...	I understand that you are still hesitating since this is a first visit. I have many customers that decide on their first visit because we take the time to go through the different concerns. Maybe there are still some concerns that we have not yet discussed?

of making a mistake, itself generates the self-protection action: delay or escape. Not taking a decision will at least not create a new problem—this is part of the customer's mindset.

To succeed in overcoming the time factor, the first important rule is to believe that, "now" is always possible.

4.8.2 Emphasize The Opportunity

John: "I might need more time to consider—Anyway, I still have time."

Henry: "Sure—and it's true that you still have a few months to become certain of your decision.

That being said, since you really like our brand and this new model we just created, will you really take more time, I shall even say 'waste time' in looking around?

You know, Mr. Hudson, that sometimes when 'it's right' it's just right!"

Another way to facilitate the time factor is to present time as a true opportunity. It is true that our affluent customers are not always able to find the right opportunity, simply because they do not have the time to search—they prefer to spend time working at their company or with their family (Table 4.8.B).

4.8.3 Create A Sense Of Urgency

John: "Since the delivery lead time is only three months, maybe I shall come back in April and we can order it then?"

Henry: "It's true that this is the normal lead time. And this model is new and as you can see it's going to be very popular. I will do my best to respect the lead time but I depend on the factory

Table 4.8.B Key words for an immediate decision

Key Words	Sales Advisor
Opportunity	"This is a true opportunity, to be the first or one of the first 'happy drivers'!"
Chance	"It's lucky that we just launched the ideal car for you."
Unique	"It's a unique offer that applies only to you, and only for today, to thank you for your decision."
Exceptional	"It's an exceptional offer since we are pre-launching only."

Table 4.8.C Reasons for deciding now

Risks	Sales Advisor
Missing out on the product	"This model might be not available anymore."
Delay	"You might have to wait a long time for delivery of this model if you delay. This model might have a very long lead time."
Time consuming	"You could well end up taking more time without finding a better option! It's time consuming and your time is very precious!"
Peace of mind	"As you have to take the decision, and if you take it now, you will have complete peace of mind. Then you can just wait for delivery of the car!"

and delivery is on a first-contract-signed, first-customer-served basis."

John: "Why don't we set the delivery now to secure your car and we can adjust later if necessary?"

As mentioned previously, the customer's self-protection tendency is to postpone the decision should they still have any small remaining doubts. Elimination of any last doubts and working on this time objection will be crucial to concluding sales, and we will extensively look at how to deal with objections later on.

Another possible way to influence decision making is to show the risk and disadvantages of not taking the decision right now – immediately! (Table 4.8.C).

4.8.4 Time Is Precious To Everyone

Time is what money cannot buy. It is precious and priceless. Affluent customers probably know this better than anyone else. They spend time wisely: investing and making money. Time is also very precious to you, their trusted sales advisor. Each client presents a true opportunity to achieve sales.

A very good sales advisor is one that believes that "now," is always possible for a customer's purchase. A less proactive sales advisor tends to believe that customers need more time to decide and that it is normal to do so. Customers need to be reassured quickly by you, in order to close the sale as soon as possible.

A very good salesperson is also one who knows when to wait and for how long. When closing a deal is not possible, and appropriate timing is not there, you should also know how to step back and prepare for the next sales opportunity with elegance and always with the special Luxury selling touch.

Voilà! We are done with the five motivational, decision making factors:

– Brand
– Product
– Price
– Place (service)
– Time

By always having these factors in mind, you become more efficient, able to reach the trigger and really influence the purchase decision.

We will investigate in the coming chapter, the Active Selling Method, and will walk you through the 7 steps of this selling process.

4.8.5   Time Is At The Last Stage of Decision Making

The customer starts by considering brand, product and price. Then it comes to the time to think about where and with whom should this crucial decision be made. Do I buy now? (Chart 4.6)

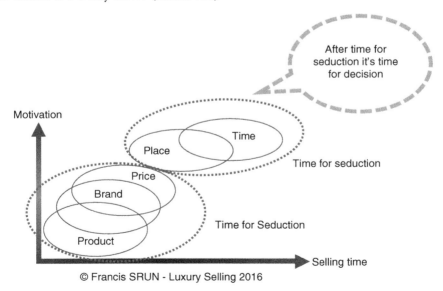

Chart 4.6   Progression of the 5 decisional factors

4.8.6 Time to Recap

At the end of this third part of *Luxury Selling* may I invite you to write a summary? It might seem old-fashioned, but if you are not able to recap now, you will probably not be able to have clear ideas later.

In the next part of the book, I will walk you through the 7 steps of the selling process. Before this journey, let us take the time for a resourceful break by sitting down and thinking back on customer's psychology. Here is the key to the objective of influencing their decision.

> ### Thinking Corner
>
> Try the white page exercise! Write a 1-page summary about customers' buying behavior. Write in a style appropriate to explain it to someone who is not a sales advisor.

5

The 7 Steps

5.1 Active Selling

5.1.1 A Roadmap To Success

When you cook, do you follow a recipe? Top chefs are always refining their culinary offerings but they base their creations on recipes. They write down each step precisely, the quantity of ingredients needed and even take photos of the various ingredients to ensure they always achieve the same best quality.

Golden Rule Corner

Selling requires creativity but also method.
Most of the time improvisation leads to failure.

Creativity takes place before the customer enters a restaurant. Improvisation on the other hand is often the shortcut to failure. A very experienced sales advisor may say: "I do not need a selling method to perform." In reality, successful sales advisors always have a selling process that they apply and integrate naturally into their everyday selling routine. It's more or less like a driver, who claims that that they do not need training to improve their driving since they are already driving.

© The Author(s) 2017
F. Srun, *Luxury Selling*, DOI 10.1007/978-3-319-45525-9_5

There is no ultimate recipe for successful selling. There are different ways to achieve success. What is for sure is that there is one certain logic, a necessary pathway from welcoming the customer into the store to the moment they leave.

What we propose here is a roadmap for success. When you are familiar with the roadmap, you can drive safely and anticipate better. And you will have a more thorough understanding of where you are in the selling process.

5.1.2 The 7 Steps to Success

Alice works in Paris. In the early morning Paris is particularly beautiful. Alice is finishing her make-up, getting herself ready to start her day in one of the most renowned jewelry boutiques. She will look great—ready to meet customers. But is she really ready? The 1st step is to be prepared to sell. Is she familiar with the new products and the various appointments for the day? Preparation is key and includes being ready mentally to start the day. Alice prepares herself by taking the time to make herself look good. She always starts her day with a big smile to herself.

A middle-aged couple (who look like they might be from America—the husband has a baseball cap) are walking along the street, looking in all the boutiques' windows. Alice notices them. A few moments later, the couple arrive outside the boutique and look in the window. Alice gives them a big smile. The couple hesitate but Alice is already walking to the door and, still smiling, opens it graciously and greets the couple with a warm *bonjour*. The couple enter the boutique and the 2nd step in the selling process begins. This is known as the welcoming stage.

Alice manages to quickly establish trust, notably by offering services and taking very good care of the visitors with sincerity. The couple are invited to take a seat which they accept. Alice has successfully navigated the 2nd step, and now prepares to sell.

She begins the 3rd step: to discover the needs of the couple. Mr. and Mrs. Taylor are looking for wedding anniversary jewelry. Alice uses her techniques to engage her customers in conversation before selecting a few creations to present, once Mrs. Taylor's personal taste has been more or less clarified.

Promptly, she moves on to the 4th step: presentation. During this important phase of the seduction process, Alice creates desire for the different creations, sharing with pride her expertise and creating romance around the creations, telling the extraordinary with simple words. Alice becomes the magician, giving life to the different creations she has presented. The Taylors are tempted but still have some doubts. As part of the 5th step, Alice understands that it's crucial that these doubts are brought to the surface so they can be alleviated. For the customer, this stage in the process is the fear phase: customers don't want to make a mistake by deciding too quickly.

During step 5, Alice will do her best to resolve their objections and even help Michelle and Allan Taylor to voice them, while also offering reassurance.

Since Alice feels that they have made a great choice and that they are ready to make the purchase, she moves to step 6 and prepares to close the sale. She knows that customers need to be assisted at the end of the buying process in order to reduce any remaining doubts.

Last but not least, after hearing their decision to purchase, Alice begins to build a long term relationship, preparing for their next visit and next purchase. And even if the customer has not made a purchase, Alice still goes through the client relationship building, in order to capitalize on the visit and prepare for future visits, thereby establishing a long term relationship. Alice, in the final 7th step, builds loyalty—the last stage in the 7 steps to success (Table 5.1.A).

Table 5.1.A The 7 steps and their objectives

Selling Step	Customer's Mindset	Sales Advisor's Objective
Preparation	Vague desire	Be ready—360°
Welcoming	Have a look—why not?	Gain trust and time for the next step
Discovering	No harm in sharing	Determine the desire and motivations
Presenting	Nice, but not sure it's the right choice	Select the right offering—seduce
Convincing	Looks okay, but not 100% sure	Alleviate objections—nicely
Closing	It cannot be the wrong choice	Help the customer to decide and make the sale
Building loyalty	Pleasure in the decision	Be sure to see the customer again

5.1.3 Active Selling

Manager's Corner

Learn from the best swimmers! After each competition, no matter what the result, you need to take time out to analyze straight away. Close your eyes and play back the entire race in your mind, from the first stroke through the first turn until the last moment when the swimmer had to make a last effort to touch the toe board at arrival. This effort of review and introspection is the key to improving and future success. As a sales advisor, after each selling session I invite you to take a deep breath, drink some water and play back the selling session you had. What went very well and what went wrong? Which step of the selling process faltered? Why?

Active selling is a method that I have defined in reaction to many selling situations that I've been in. It's also the fruit of experience from the observation of the selling process with any Luxury and/or any high price product. It actually can be applied to all kinds of products, when a true customer decision is necessary. The idea is to understand, to be in control and to be able to progress. A sales advisor that practices active selling will be AWARE, whereas a passive sales advisor is not clear of his/her own practices (Table 5.1.B).

We will see that on top of having control of the situation by mastering the 7 steps, and by focusing on the 5 decision making motivational factors you can be very efficient in influencing and helping your customers to decide (Table 5.1.C):

- Brand, Product, Price, Place, Time

Table 5.1.B Active/passive selling

	Confidence	Control	Conversion
Passive selling	Lack of self-confidence causes more stress: especially with difficult customers.	Less able to navigate a visit through the necessary steps. Risk of losing easy customers.	Less conversion mainly due to the sales advisor's strong desire to conclude. Not able to explain sales successes or missed sales opportunities.
Active selling	Self-confidence. Able to handle all situations.	Able to accomplish all the steps and increase opportunity to conclude a sale positively.	High conversion through carefully dealing with customers, step-by-step. Able to explain each sale and analyze any missed sales.

Table 5.1.C Active selling

Active Selling	The Five Decision Making Motivational Factors
The 7 Steps	Sell by following a rational selling pattern in 7 steps and based on the customer's 5 decision making motivational factors

5.1.4   The Road To Active Selling

To engage in active selling, energy is the first requirement. With time, a sales advisor can learn how to mobilize this energy and increase their selling skill. Too much energy without selling skill only leads to a pushy selling style. Skill without energy is not sufficient: passive selling never brings about the best results (Chart 5.1).

5.1.5   Be Intelligent!

Recent research has pointed out different types of intelligence. Selling intelligence is most likely a combination of the capacity to understand situations (rationally but also emotionally), a certain capacity to analyze

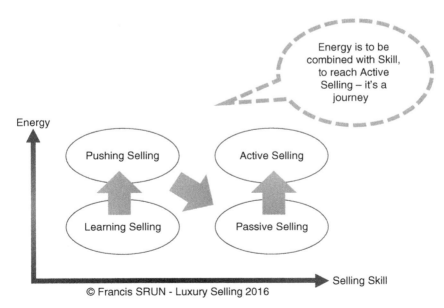

Chart 5.1   Dynamic selling skill

and understand the customer's desires and fears (you learn by experience) and an ability to deliver and interact with customers.

The best sales advisors are never arrogant. Being humble, approachable and affable are other signs of intelligence.

5.1.6 Be Creative!

I have had the chance to meet and observe many sales advisors as a client, a reporting line Manager and as a trainer. I am always amazed by the creativity of sales advisors. This creativity can be expressed in humor. But the ability to find solutions and reassure the customer during the phase of doubt and fear is another form of creative expression.

> ### Golden Rule
> Be creative in the selling process. There is a logical approach to selling but the true difference is creativity. Believe in your own intelligence.

In the sections that follow, we walk through the active selling method, focusing on the persuasive approach and the 5 decision making motivational factors. We will also take the necessary time to analyze each motivational factor to fully understand them and be able to use them to influence customers effectively.

5.2   Step 1: Preparing

Let's start the journey with a story:

> ### Story Corner
> Master Wang is a famous Chinese artist and is known for his paintings of fruit and flowers. A renowned French vineyard owner placed an order for four paintings, with the theme of grapes representing the four seasons. After a few months, Master Wang still had not delivered the works. The owner became worried and wondered whether Master Wang was working on them. Master Wang replied that he was and insisted on delivering the

paintings himself. He arrived and spent one full day walking in the vineyard. "Tomorrow," he said to the owner, "tomorrow, I will show you the paintings." The next day, Master Wang installed himself at a table, with all his materials: brush, Chinese ink, some water and so forth. He invited the owner to join him. In silence and quite effectively, he realized the four pieces of art in less than thirty minutes. "Very impressive and beautiful, Master Wang. They are also probably the most expensive grapes in history, especially looking at the time needed to produce them!" the owner added. "It is quick to draw them," answered Master Wang, "but each grain of the grape needed thirty years of practice, patience and perseverance to be produced, just like your wines," he concluded with a large smile.

5.2.1 Competence

In this section, we will not elaborate upon retail preparation such as merchandising, displaying and all the other actions needed for the store to be ready for customers. We will focus on the sales advisor's own preparation: to be ready to sell, in terms of competence (or the ability to sell).

When we say a sales advisor is competent, we mean that person can sell, and can sell in various situations and to different types of clients. Competent sales advisors can adapt quickly to new products, new clients and a new commercial environment. The capacity to adapt to product, clients and any situation are the true qualities of skillful selling. Can you imagine a car driver who is only able to drive on motorways? A true driver is able to drive on any road, under any weather conditions, safely. A competent driver will also quickly adapt his skill when driving a new car, by adjusting his driving in response to the performance of the new car.

Selling competence is even more complex: each customer is different; they buy different kinds of product and have different motivations. And, there is no second chance; sales advisors need to succeed and reach their goal by adapting very quickly to the client and the selling situation (Table 5.2.A).

Selling competence requires different skills:

– Knowledge
– Know-how
– Attitude

Table 5.2.A The 3 components of competency

		Car	Insurance
Knowledge	What I need to know to sell	Car functions, specifics, similar competitively priced cars, benefits compared to competition.	Financial instruments, similar competitive products, product benefits compared to competition.
Know-how	How to sell	Listen to customer's real motivation, handle price bargaining, conclude sale.	Listen to the customer's real motivation. Explain in very simple ways. Reassure.
Attitude	The way I sell	Gain trust and be seen as a reliable person, and able to help.	Gain trust and more: become the financial friend/advisor of the family.

The only way to acquire competency is to be active: practice, experiment.

Golden Rule Corner

Know at least as much as your clients!
Know your company's official and published information: that's the minimum.
Know their possible public information source and check it: that's a must.

5.2.2 Knowledge Preparation

Nowadays there is a huge range of information of various depth and breadth. Anyone who takes the necessary time and acts with sufficient skill can become an expert, thanks to the new Information Age. The challenge is no longer about how to access information, but how to transform information into knowledge. It's about selection, organization of the information, and integration into one's daily professional selling life.

• Makes notes

It sounds old-fashioned and appears odd to many, but nothing can replace taking notes, summarizing and synthesizing information. It is important that the words become yours, and are written in the way that you would say them—in your voice. With practice, you will become better at taking good notes. And your notes will become shorter and more concise, gaining more precision each time. Shorter notes often result in your ability to be concise and clear for the customers who are going to listen to you.

Golden Rule Corner

"What you know is only what you can tell."
"The more you tell the better you can tell."
"The more you tell the more you know."

• Memorize as much as you can

Story Corner

At a global meeting of car sales advisors, the trainer asked the participants how they manage pricing information. An American said: "We have an iPad; all the prices are on it." A British sales advisor smiled and said: "What happens if your iPad runs out of battery? We still use a printed folder and that never runs out of power." The Japanese sales advisor commented: "The folder is too big and you cannot always have it with you...We made a small booklet with all the prices and that booklet is in every sales advisor's pocket." The Chinese sales advisor said: "Well, we try to remember all the prices by heart. You always have your head with you."

What is most important is the ability to find information quickly, and to be accurate. The best advisors always make the effort. Memorization brings true peace of mind and allows you to focus on other subjects. This peace of mind can be enhanced further by having trustworthy tools to fall back on, such as an iPad, a folder or a pocket booklet. It is important to always have them to hand, and not to have to look for them. Some might find this approach "old school" but I recommend that you try to remember the maximum amount of information and, if necessary, double-check it on your preferred support tool. When you have memorized the information, you are more tranquil—needing only to double-check if more precision is needed and to avoid making a mistake.

• Create your own tools

5.2.3 Know-how Preparation

To be able to sell better, sales advisors should of course be trained and coached and many companies do provide comprehensive training programs. But the best sales advisors do not only follow the corporate program. They are able to find their own ways to train and prepare for better selling. Let's see what the best practices for self-preparation are.

- Learning from colleagues

An English tea merchant offered me this beautiful story:

> ### Story Corner
>
> "As a merchant, I import from India and buy from different tea producers. There is one producer in particular that I always have a great pleasure to visit because the hospitality is great. During the different tea tasting, selection process and negotiations, there is one young man who everyone calls "Tea Boy." He is there to help pull the water, change teas and is always smiling and available during all the buying sessions. At all times, Tea Boy was there and patiently assisted us.
>
> One day, I arrived at the office and was greeted by Tea Boy, who was dressed in an immaculate suit. "Well! Tea Boy, you got a promotion! Congratulations!" "Yes, Sir, I have in fact been promoted to the position of Commercial Director."
>
> "Actually, it's my father, the owner of this company, who had this idea...He asked me to learn how to converse with buyers by learning from the different sales persons...And, I did actually did learn a lot during the last two years of serving tea. He was right." "Well," I asked him, "how does your father know that you are ready to sell?" The new Director said with a large smile: "Actually, he made his decision based on the quality of tea I managed to make!"

Each of your colleagues holds the keys to best practices for acquiring know-how: proven success keys. They are better than any other advice than I can ever offer you, simply owing to the fact that in your own selling environment you can test what works, how it works and can therefore learn very quickly. This book will help you recognize the key to learning from your colleagues, by alerting you to what to observe. The best way to learn from each other is to assist each other.

- Learn from the competition

It is also very interesting to learn from competition and it's free! You have double the benefits at no additional training cost. The first benefit is that you can be in the shoes of the customer. As a customer, were you welcomed properly and spoken to in the same way as you have been practicing? How did it make you feel? How do you feel about the way the sales advisor dealt with your objections—were you be convinced? The second benefit comes from learning the selling techniques of your competition and bench-marking them against your own practices.

• Learning from different industries

You can also be inspired by other types of product and service. As a car seller observe how a watch seller works and compare their techniques with your own practices. There are certainly many ideas that can be borrowed from other selling professionals.

By being curious and taking the time to observe, you can learn a surprising amount from different industries even those that you had not imagined you could learn from.

We certainly do not recommend the following selling process, yet we can still learn from what we observe. The carpet merchant:

1. Raised the client's interest quickly (not easy in a touristic place, lack of time)
2. Allowed the client to first select the product
3. Presented the product
4. Negotiated the price

5.2.4 Preparation For Knowing How To Behave

Having sufficient knowledge and selling techniques are not enough to sell. As discussed, inspiring trust is key and so is having the correct attitude.

Having the right attitude in selling to customers can first be perceived in your non-verbal expression/communication: the way you stand, move, smile and look at the customer. The correct attitude for selling to customers also means having the ability to be seen as knowledgeable, positive, helpful, trustworthy, elegant and so on. It requires the capacity to generate a positive feeling in the customer. It means the bringing together of many components—of many factors. It's more or less about how you express yourself with your body language. The way you:

- Present yourself
- Speak
- Move
- Look at the customer
- Interact with others

The main preparation for this selling behavior is more complex. The 1st idea is to be fully aware of the importance of your attitude, especially during Luxury selling. In the beginning of the book, I prepared you extensively for this.

The 2nd need is to have a permanent awareness of self. During a selling session, imagine yourself on a stage. Be at the "meta-position" level and look at yourself constantly. Be conscious of the way you smile, move and behave. Make the necessary corrections and slowly you will progress.

Manager's Corner

One of the key tools to develop further sales competency is to create the habit of taking the "meta-position". Ask your team members to observe themselves during debriefing after a selling session. Sales advisors have to try and remember what happened. They will become increasingly conscious about their selling process, even while they are selling. This ability to see one's self (meta-position) is key to self-development in selling skills.

You can also learn, be inspired by the hospitality industries. I encourage sales advisors to experience 5-star hotels or Parisian palaces, not necessarily by staying at them but by perhaps having breakfast or supper at one of these venues to allow you to spend some quality time observing and learning from the service you received.

But the really important qualities of behavior, that is, sincerity and positivity, can only come from a sincere and positive mindset. Consider the boutique, the salon and the selling space as a stage. A person on stage is performing for others, with the obligation to forget about oneself. It is not only about being professional. It is also about being generous toward your customers, encouraging them to actively seek you out during a visit.

Competence is the capacity to always be able to perform through adaptation. Three components are necessary for this competence: knowledge, know-how and attitude.

The best sales advisors are those who are able to achieve the right balance within and between these three dimensions.

At the end of Step 1, your competencies are fully prepared and you are ready to face any customer.

5.3   Step 2: Welcoming

Lisa enters the Italian fashion store and browses through the various bags. Rather than following Lisa too closely, Lucy simply greeted her warmly when she walked into the store, thereby spontaneously inviting the customer to follow her.

> *Lucy*:   "Good afternoon Madame."
> After Lisa had stepped inside the boutique, Lucy approached her again:
> *Lucy*:   "Welcome to *Maison M*, Madame. Thank you for coming to visit us."
> *Lucy*:   "It's such a hot day, may I offer you some refreshment first?"
> *Lucy*:   "Oh, no thank you. I am just looking…"
> *Lucy*:   "Please take your time and I will be around to assist you."
> *Lisa*:   "It seems that you have a new bag that is very in fashion these days."
> *Lucy*:   "My compliments, Madame. Yes, we do have a new bag everyone talks about!"
> *Lisa*:   "Let me walk you to our iconic Bag B. This way please."
> Lucy leads the way and walks Lisa to the display of handbags.

A Luxury boutique, a high-end car showroom and a private banking office are not places that one goes every day, even for affluent customers, simply because they do not need to. These places can also be new to them, like the sales team. It is rather like going to someone's home when you do not know the person and they don't know you. You are not expected and you are afraid to disturb them. The unknown is never comfortable. Many sales advisors forget this first mental stress for customers, as they are used to their own boutiques and feel at ease, as though they were at home.

The thick carpet, the marble, the merchandise and the large smile of the sales associate suggest that you had better be able to afford the products and make a purchase! It is not necessarily intimidating to all customers, but certainly it can be for many.

Customers need some desire to motivate them to enter the store: to look, to understand, to possibly find a product they are thinking about and so forth.

They never, or very rarely come in with the firm intention to buy. This is why a good welcome is key. You need to offer a genuine welcome in order to establish trust, gain the customer's time and allow the advising and selling process to begin.

5.3.1 Welcome Genuinely

When a good friend visits you, the first reaction should be joy. The second would be pleasure. To truly welcome someone, you need to demonstrate this joy by a simple and very warm welcoming "Good Morning," for example, much as you would a friend, or someone who is taking his precious time to visit you.

As a second step, I recommend a more formal welcome that identifies and creates a connection for your customer to your brand or boutique. This is a very natural approach. The key is to show your appreciation and pleasure in seeing your customer, as you would a friend: "Welcome to *Maison M*, Madame."

Would you ask your good friend why he is coming to see you? It would be impolite, even rude. In reality, however, this very often sales advisors do ask customers why they are visiting: "How can I help you?"

Or worse, they will even ask if the customer wants to make a purchase or not: "Is there anything you have noticed, and how can I help you?"

The customer's reaction is very often one of self-protection:

"It's okay."
"I'm just looking."
"It's fine, thank you."

> **Golden Rule Corner**
>
> Don't ask questions that never bring good answers.

I do not believe that you need to "break the ice." Quite simply, from the beginning there is no ice to break but only common ground to find. This is what I call a fundamental misunderstanding, as illustrated below (Table 5.3.A):

Table 5.3.A Phase and customer's mindset

Phase	Customer's Mindset	Sales Advisor's Mindset
Decision to enter the store	Let's enter but just to look, not to buy.	A customer is entering. Great—I have to sell.
After entering the store	Let's look first.	Let's see what the customer wants!
Looking at the products	Let's see—there's no harm looking around.	Need to find out what the customer wants to buy so as to not miss the selling time.
Finding an interesting product	Let's check the product—you never know.	The customer has found a product. Need to do a good presentation and sell it.

You remember Paul Morgan? The welcoming process also applies to an office meeting:

Roger:	"Good morning, Mr. Morgan!"
Paul Morgan:	"Morning, sorry for being late for the appointment."
Roger:	"Thank you for coming to Bank B, it's great that you made it."
Roger:	"Mr. Morgan—This is our Good Morning Menu. Please tell me what would be your choice! By the way, our coffee is particular nice, with quite a large selection."
Paul:	"That's nice. A coffee and some chocolate cookies would do. Thank you—I didn't have time for breakfast this morning."
Paul:	"Thank you, I recently received some investment plan proposals and would just like to understand them better."
Roger:	"Certainly, Mr. Morgan, and be assured that my only objective today is having you fully understand our personal long-term, financial gain solutions."
Paul:	"And, I have to admit that it's not always easy to comprehend."
Roger:	"We need to take the necessary time to explain everything. I really appreciate you coming to see me so that we can have a conversation around the subject!"

To truly welcome a customer, forget about selling. The best way to "break the ice" is to not have any ice—the buying obligation. You need to acknowledge that a customer entering the store is not necessarily coming in to buy (at least initially). And as a method of self-protection, a customer rarely comes in with the decision to buy today. Instead of having that too quick and immediate selling objective (when you have this, the customer can feel it and, with reason, will be even more cautious), enjoy the pleasure of the encounter.

Golden Rule Corner

To truly welcome a customer, do it genuinely. Forget about the sales for the moment and enjoy the encounter.

5.3.2 Service To Gain Trust

There is always a way to truly offer good service to your customer.

When a sales advisor asks his customer "How I can help you?" or "Is there any product you would like to see?" these are not questions designed to help but rather a selling proposal. Put yourself in the customer's shoes (Table 5.3.B):

Respecting the customer's freedom to "just look" will create immediate trust and establish a more relaxed atmosphere. Of course, sales advisors do need to sell but instead of thinking they need to achieve this quickly, they should try to welcome the customer appropriately. There is no shortcut to this and it requires treating everyone in the best possible manner (Table 5.3.C).

Instead of proposing a service, why not simply help, assist and provide true service to the customer?

Table 5.3.B Customer's reserved attitude

	Customer's Understanding	Customer's Reaction
How can I help you?	What do I want to buy?	I am just looking.
How can I assist you?	What do I want to see?	I am just looking around—not yet.
Is there any product you would like to see?	Is there any product I would like to buy?	No, I am just looking.
Is there any specific product you have in mind?	What do I want to buy?	I am just looking.

Table 5.3.C Services to offer

Offer of Service	Examples
Lighten the customer's load	"Can I help you with your shopping bags? I can keep them here for you and we will keep an eye on them."
Drinks	"This is our beverages menu, Madame. We have choices of tea, juices and soft drinks, and of course we also make a good Italian coffee!"
Special attention to customers' children	"Welcome to you young lady. Would you like a refreshing juice? We also have some books there for you to read. Or would you prefer a drawing activity?"
Extra services	"Milan traffic is heavy especially in summer and I hope you had no difficulty finding a taxi. If you need any help with transportation we have special taxi drivers that we know and they will always make themselves available."

5.3.3 Show Concern and Interest

It's always possible to show concern for your visitor:
"It's very hot today in Milan. Please do be sure to drink enough water, especially your children."
"The weather forecast is for very heavy rain tomorrow, so please be careful!"

And also express interest in your visitor:
"You look like such a friendly person, Madame. May I ask you where you are from?"
"If I guess that you are American, am I right?"

At last, do not forget that well-placed compliments are always welcome and increase positive feelings:
"You look so nice that I must compliment you sincerely, Madame."
"You inspire me, Madame, with all your grace. My compliments, Madame."

5.3.4 Retain Your Customer

In my experience, if customers leave the store during the welcoming stage, it's never because they don't find what they are looking for. It's simply because the sales advisor was not able to retain their visitors.

- Exclusive sales advisor

Customers leave the store or boutique if they are not able to establish contact with a sales advisor. I recommend that you quickly establish a sales advisor-to-client, one-to-one protocol. Clients need to feel they are being valued and have someone to talk to.

- Retaining services

Many services contribute to your warm welcoming and allow you to retain customers. A coffee or tea creates time and a customer will need to wait for it. Chinese customers love Chinese tea, especially when they travel. Europeans like espresso, and usually will ask for another after the first one. Providing some confectionery, biscuits or cakes also contributes to the pleasure of staying.

The most powerful and easy retaining service is table hospitality. The selling table becomes a coffee table, a dinner table. Offer a menu with different choices. A drink, whether hot or cold, is part of the expected minimum gesture. And since everyone is doing the same, why not do it better—that is, deliver the highest possible standard.

Story Corner

There is an expression in French qualifying a resilient sales person as a "marchand de tapis" meaning literally carpet merchant. I met one in Tunisia. After I entered his boutique and looked at the different carpets on display, the owner came in with a big silver tray, with tea and very appealing oriental cakes. I turned down the nice Oriental teatime offer and prepared to leave. He told me that this is his pleasure and that a mint tea prepared must be tasted and he would be so grateful for my acceptance of his hospitality. I sat down and he described all the different kind of cakes, one by one. He was patient enough not to show me the carpets as I expected him to do until he noticed that I had my eyes on a carpet hanging on the wall. He asked his assistant to display it on the floor and said: "To appreciate a carpet, you need to see it from the right angle. Let me tell you the story of this one..."

One of the most frequent mistakes is to think that the customer's time is limited and therefore you had better get to the selling process as soon as possible. To welcome warmly and offer good hospitality are part of the selling process and most often the easiest things to deliver successfully, quite simply because a customer rarely refuses the offer of a drink—and many even expect to receive one.

A second possible retaining service is to have customer try the product. In Luxury fashion, for example, a customer trying on a suit or a pair of shoes must remain in the boutique. The same is true when trying on a Luxury watch or an item of jewelry: keeping the customer busy trying the product is a very good way of retaining the customer.

—Get the customer's attention

> *Lucy*: "Madame, I am not sure if you noticed our iconic leather creation, the Bag B, displayed over there?"
>
> *Alice*: "Oh Madame, I should of course introduce this new creation to you! It just arrived and I would love to hear your opinion of it."

—Orient your customer

By being in the right place in the boutique, you can engage with the customer at different moments of their visit. If you stand in a certain place in the boutique, customers will most certainly choose to head in another direction so as to avoid the sales advisor. By guiding the customer and walking them in a certain direction, effectively leading the customer in the direction the sales advisor wants them to go, sales advisor does not really give the customer a choice and most of the time they manage to orient them.

—Avoid customers leaving

By being alert and strategically positioned (not too far from the door), sales advisors can prevent clients wanting to leave by leading them to another part of the store that the customer might have missed or toward a new collection for their review.

—Make the customer take a seat

This is a main key to success. A seated customer spends three times more money compared to a customer who is standing. To encourage a customer to take a seat, integrate sitting as part of the selling advising process. It has to seem natural. Always pull out the chair for the customer and wait until the customer sits down.

The objective to achieve at the end of Step 2 is to have the customer agree to stay for a full presentation. A second objective is to establish a positive and warm relationship. These are only the objectives and this is already a lot, if not essential. Without the ability to retain customers, a sales advisor never has the chance to sell!

We will see in the next section how to discover the customer's desire, and also understand customer's fears and doubts.

5.4   Step 3: Discovering

5.4.1 Discover Subtlety

Martial: "Mr. Wang, thank you for taking time to appreciate our new collections."

Martial: "I am sure that you have heard about our brand…May I ask you if this is the first time you have visited us?"

Peter: "Yes…I have never seen your timepieces in person. It happens that I have few hours before I go to Lausanne."

Martial: "Lausanne must be so nice with this summer weather! Thank you for giving me this opportunity."

Peter: "May I know if you already had a specific model in mind, that you would like to examine first?"

Peter: "Not really, just show me a few pieces to start with."

Martial: "Certainly! If you come to us, it means that you are a connoisseur…Am I right?"

Peter: "Oh, I love timepieces!"

Martial: "I was sure—just from looking at the excellent piece on your wrist."

Peter: "We have quite a large collection…Would you like to focus on different movements or do you have a specific idea in mind already?"

Peter:	"I appreciate a good mechanical movement, for sure."
Martial:	"Excellent—I shall first I introduce you to three of our *manufacture* movements."

As I mentioned in earlier chapters, there is a tremendous difference between a client and a buyer. A professional buyer always has a book of specs, a budget, a time line and, more importantly, an obligation to buy. While, for a customer, there is never a clear expectation (but sometimes there is one that exists unconsciously), rarely an existing budget, no real time line and the customer has no obligation to buy. A wedding anniversary gift could be a beautiful diamond necklace, or a pearl one, or even something totally different such as a 1-week private yachting vacation.

In B-to-B selling, salesmen will simply elicit the different expectations from the different buyers, list them and answer with proposals, most of the time, in another meeting. Here, there is no possibility, no time and no another chance to propose.

In B-to-C, since the customer is not really clear yet about his own desire, expectations cannot help you to tell what they really want. Some do not always play the transparency game—as a self-protection method from buying and in order to deliberately not divulge their desires.

For all these reasons, this important step is called "discovering." It means that you need a subtle approach with the customer, to discover what is not obvious at first glance.

Why is Peter Wang here, in Geneva, today and in this boutique here and now? A first, and way too off-handed answer, would be "just looking" or "taking the opportunity to have a look." Certainly—and this is fine—but why? Why would Mr. Wang be willing to spend some of his precious time looking at timepieces? Why not at something else? There are many others brands around. Why would he be looking today rather than taking some rest before his next flight or train?

Customers' available time can be limited and they do not always shop or take the liberty to browse. Mr. Wang cannot spend all his time looking at all the available brands of timepieces. He cannot spend time looking at all the items that he may be interested in because he is a well occupied businessman.

By coming into a retail boutique, he is already expressing an intention to discover.

5.4.2 There Are Always Desires, Motivations

Customers do vote with their feet! When a customer says "just looking," some sales advisors translate this into "not buying" and "do not disturb." They therefore leave the customer to browse independently and allow them to leave the store with little or no further contact. Never think that your customer is just looking. And, by the way, "just looking" is already very good! In fact, "just looking" means "I don't want to buy and you don't need to take care of me too much—just let me look and that will be fine." It's only a way for the customer to not disappoint the sales advisor, and to be left in peace when looking at the products.

Now, why would a customer just look if they don't have a sliver of desire to buy? Why would they be looking at your brand and your products among so many other brands and products?

Golden Rule Corner

There is always an intention that deserves your full attention!

The intentions of an existing client are different from those of a new client to the brand (Table 5.4.A).

- Existing client of the brand

Existing customers, are often part of the same world but deserve very individual treatment. You need to show this right away—recognize the customer, thank them nicely. This creates an immediate connection.

"Oh, you are wearing our brand. So lovely, and of course, you know us!"
"It's great to have you appreciating us because we need more clients like you."

- New visitor to the brand

A new visitor to the brand deserves attention and needs specific care. There is always some reluctance to confess their ignorance. You need to be able to speak to them at the correct level, without lecturing. It's all about sharing the right quantity of information.

"Welcome to our brand! It's so nice to have you discover who we are!"
"Thank you so much for taking the time to come and see who we are!"

Table 5.4.A Understand new/existing customers

	Already A Client Of The Brand	New To The Brand
Brand	Comfortable. Sense of belonging. Understand the brand. Share pride in the brand. Stay informed.	Learn more about a brand their entourage knows and that people talk about. Check if the brand is worth buying.
Product	Comfortable personal choice. See new models. Stay informed. Show pride. Check new collections.	See features for themselves. Discover the products from a known brand. Check the advantages. Looking for a *coup de foudre* or love at first sight product!
Price	Check prices. Check for increases. Look for promotions.	Check price level. See if prices are within budget range. Check prices correspond to value.
Place	Feel at home. Share passion. Build relationship with the sales advisor. Spend quality time.	Discover a new place. See if I can meet a good sales advisor. Spend quality time.
Time	Keep a relationship with the brand. Check for opportunities.	Shopping is quality time. Hoping for a lucky experience (special promotion, unique offering and so forth).

5.4.3 Discover Whose Decision

One of the first elements to discover is who is going to take the decision. It is not always very obvious even though it is key to understand who is who in any sales transaction. In fact, there are four potential decision makers that must be taken into consideration:

- Decision maker: This may appear to be obvious, but can be tricky to determine.
- Who is paying: It's very often a different person from the decision maker.
- Who will use the product: It's very often a different person from the person who pays.
- Veto person: They can say no.

During the phase of welcoming, you must build trust with all visitors. This is especially the case with a group—beware of the individuals and if possible identify their role. The one who is going to make the decision is not necessarily the one who will pay.

For Mrs. and Mr. Taylor it is quite clear that Mrs. Taylor's "yes" will get approval from her husband. Even for a property purchase in the case of the

Williams, Sophie's role is at the center of the decision. She can say no—as she is the one who has to live in the property more often than Thomas. She can also say no if she doesn't like the property and is quite sure that Thomas will not insist too much. Sophie most likely has better judgment, being the one who is most likely to take the lead in decorating and arranging their new home.

It is crucial therefore to be conscious of a customer's spouse and children when they visit together. Typically, Asian customers have a deep respect for their parents, and elder visitors hold the "right to veto" and quite often don't hesitate to use it when they consider that the products are not worth buying (Chart 5.2).

Look at Chart 5.2 and consider the example of Mrs. and Mr. Taylor visiting Paris to find a piece of wedding anniversary jewelry. Mr. Taylor is evidently the person who will pay but he's not the sole decision maker when he is visiting the store with Mrs. Taylor. If he were alone, he would be the only decision maker, while his wife Michelle would be in the background of the decision as the recipient of the gift. Michelle is the one who is going to use the jewelry, but she also wears it for her husband and therefore would not make a decision without her husband liking the item.

Michelle has the right to veto: even if Allan likes a particular piece, she could simply say no. On the other hand, even if Allan didn't really like her choice, he would most likely not use his right to veto the decision. His desire is to please Michelle.

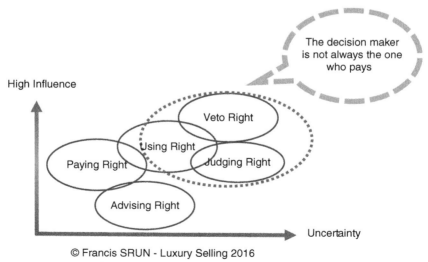

© Francis SRUN - Luxury Selling 2016

Chart 5.2   The decision makers

In a quick analysis, an expert sales advisor would know:

Decision: Michelle and Allan
Paying: Allan
Using: Michelle but needs Allan's appreciation
Veto: Michelle

The best option would be to focus on Michelle and work to get Allan on board.
Is Mrs. Taylor familiar with the brand? What kind of jewelry does she already have? For her, what is an exceptional piece in terms of price? All the necessary questions have to be raised, focusing only on Michelle, even if her self-confident husband looks like he is able to take the decision alone.

The situation can be much more complicated when clients visit with friends who are there to offer their opinion. It could also be the case that grand-parents and children are involved.

5.4.4 Observe Discreetly

When a customer enters a store, he is naturally greeted by a sales advisor. No matter what, the customer feels like he's being observed. The sales advisor's first challenge is to put the customer at ease and not allow the customer to have the very unpleasant feeling of being watched.

To avoid staring at the customer, the easiest method is to move around the boutique. After a warm greeting, the sales advisor could move slowly, keeping himself available for the customer but not placing himself immediately next to the customer. After making friendly eye contact, the sales advisor can avert his gaze and thereby release the customer from the feeling of being observed.

Everything is in the eye contact of the sales advisor. If you look seriously at the customer, he will immediately feel not only like he is being observed but, even worse, like he is being judged. When you look at a customer, especially at the beginning of his visit, always smile.

Expert sales advisors are trained and always manage to quickly elicit some initial messages from the customer through their early observations (Table 5.4.B).

Table 5.4.B Customer observation

	What To Observe	Client's Possible Expression
Dress code	The way a customer dresses always tells you something—not everything, but still something to be aware of.	"This is ME."
Accessories	The accessories are never there by chance: they express a clear intention. They are codes to decode.	"This who I want to be."
Eye contact	What are customers looking at? How does a customer make eye contact with the boutique's sales advisors?	"This how I want to interact."
Physical expression	How the customer moves: Note the changes that occur during the visit	Tensions, pleasures, desires and fears.

Observations are natural and useful, but can also be dangerous if interpreted and used incorrectly. When a customer comes to a shoe store wearing sneakers/trainers, what could this mean? It will mean something only if placed into context with the other information and messages you will receive.

5.4.5 Listen Actively

You need to imagine the conversation as a space. In this space, there must be silence. And, it cannot be too heavy—we are in Luxury selling. Depth and speed cannot offer all the necessary pleasure. The words in this space must be precise, elegant and pleasant. This space also belongs to your clients, not only to you the sales advisor. Many sales advisors feel the need to fill up this space with their rhetoric. To be able to listen, you need to provide space and the possibility for the customer to speak out.

In this free space, the invitation to take over the conversation is precisely the silence that you know how to place; this silence is the punctuation. When placed at the right moment it becomes, with intention, the time to let customers join the conversation. When you want a customer to carry on, **pause**, smile and simply wait. You will be surprised by how happy your customer is to be able to talk.

Active listening means that when you listen to your customer, you are not only taking in the information but are able to clarify and classify it. The easy rule: WHAT to WHY.

> Golden Rule Corner
>
> From WHAT to WHY. From what a customer tells you, transform it directly into WHY he is telling you this in order to be able to ACT.

5.4.6 Question Strategically

Most likely anyone reading this book will have heard about open questions and closed questions. Open questions call for elaborated answers while closed questions call for yes or no answers. In reality, the most important type of question is related not only to the form but also to the subject: what you are questioning, how you formulate your question and when you do it. I recommend a variety of formulations and to always place these questions strategically in the conversation.

I would like to invite you to go the extra mile by questioning artfully and appropriately.

Questioning is the best way to elicit relevant answers, but there are constraints that are not so easy to navigate. You are never sure that a customer will answer you sincerely or fully. To be able to maximize the value of the answers, your questions have to be (Table 5.4.C):

– Few—not too many to answer
– Easy to answer
– Pleasing to answer

In a nutshell, the more a customer is willing to answer, the better the answers you will receive. The more precise your question is, the better the potential answer.

- Focus on the customer's decision making factors

At the right moment, lead the customer to reveal the five decision making motivational factors

- Be vague when you have time to listen

It is sometimes necessary to be vague in your questioning. This approach is more an invitation to express one's self on a certain subject, rather than a question.

Table 5.4.C Discover questioning

	Key Zone To Discover	Possible Questions
Brand	Existing knowledge about the brand	I am very curious to know how you perceive our brand.
Product	Product characteristics	We have a large collection. Are there any clues being given by the customer that will allow me to more precisely propose the right product selection?
Price	Budget	For this important acquisition, maybe you already have a budget range in mind?
Place	Purchase location	Is it the first time you are visiting us? Have you already been to another of our boutiques, somewhere else in the world?
Time	Decision time frame	Do you have a specific target time frame for the decision?

Learn more about the customer's situation:

Alice: "It's such a good idea to celebrate your wedding anniversary in Paris… it's so romantic."

- Be sharp when you need a precise answer

On the opposite end of the spectrum, it is very useful to come forward with very precise questions in order to progress and be able to better understand your customer and their decision.

To learn if customers are also looking to choose a ring or a necklace:

Alice: "For this beautiful celebration jewelry, I understand that for the moment you have in mind a necklace. Maybe I can also propose beautiful rings for your consideration?"

- Be gentle because you are a nice person

The way you formulate the question determines the quality of the answer you will receive. Be gentle, be polite, be considerate. It's about a pleasure. To be able to make the purchase your customer needs this sentiment to be taken into consideration, and not questioned or challenged. Keep this in mind especially because customers do not always know what they want and therefore could find it tiring to answer questions.

- Be soft—it's about education and courtesy

To soften the questioning, you can use "pre" polite expressions or "post" polite ones.

Pre-polite expressions:
"If this is fine with you, may I know…?"
"I would be really grateful if you would tell me…?"

Post-polite expressions:
"I wonder when you will be able to take this decision—I would be so grateful if you could give me an estimated time frame."
"'I wonder how you feel about this necklace—I would really appreciate it if you would tell me your view."

5.4.7 Test Prudently

- Put out feelers

Alice:	"Madame, please let me introduce a few necklaces from various creative angles. Please tell me if you like them. We will certainly take more time to select the right creation for you."
Alice:	"Mr. Mason, please let me summarize the 5 types of long-term financial plans. Please just give me your first thoughts—that will be helpful to me to better customize the most appropriate option for you."

A feeler should always be there to help a customer clarify their initial desire. A feeler is without risk, being light and with a "just to see" factor.

- Tending temptation

Peter:	"Mr. Wang, I know that you told me that you are very keen on movement quality. Please allow me to present a new collection from our creator. It might not be what you expect in terms of the internal mechanism but the design is very strong and remains pure and clean. I would love to hear your views, as an expert timepieces collector."
Henry:	"Mr. Hudson, I can see that you already have a model in mind! Since you are here, how about taking a glance at one specific model that I would like you to see because I am quite sure that you haven't seen it yet. This beauty joined us just a few days ago."

A temptation is more pushy and progressive than a feeler. It has the benefit of being seen as a service. Through it, the sales advisor can also demonstrate their understanding of the customer.

- Progress with words

> *Alice*:   "Mrs. Taylor, I guess that for the moment you only have a necklace in mind?"
>
> *Roger*:   "Paul, I am considering now that your investment time frame is 20 years?"

During the conversation, you can "place" affirmations while making eye contact with the customer and smiling. If the customer does not disagree, it means that he agrees: silence is consent!

5.4.8 The Art Of Discovery

The best way to discover is to:

- Focus on the right person
- Take into consideration all possible decision making parties
- Mind the 5 decision making motivational factors
- Learn the different possible methods, not only questioning
- Excel in questioning but don't abuse
- Combine different ways to discover

Let's also be humble: a customer visit can be short and you have to balance the need to know with the necessity to get to the next stage, to present the product you have to sell.

The objective is not to know everything but to reach the crystallization point—that is, when you feel that their desire is now crystal clear and when you have the impression that you know what to propose and how to progress. And remain humble: you only know a portion of the story within this initial discovery and exploration phase.

Golden Rule Corner

You discover but never fully uncover the customer's desires. The different messages you manage to receive are valuable but alone are never sufficient to conclude a sale.

5.4.9 Propose

Alice:	"Mrs. and Mr. Taylor, I think I'm starting to know what might be right for you. Thank you for sharing with me. I am very impressed. Let me get the help of my colleague, Alexandre, and we will prepare a nice selection for you to review."
Roger:	"Paul, I am pretty clear about your long-term objectives. Thank you so much. Please let me introduce to you two solutions that I foresee."

To end the discovering phase, the sales advisor can use different ways to express and invite customer to enter the presentation phase. Here are two final recommendations before we consider the next step:

– Thank your customer for telling you so many things
– Compliment the customer on what you learned from them

Now you have a better idea of the customer's desire. Suddenly and logically the reason for the customer's visit today seems clear and you have a possible roadmap: what to present and how to present.

In the next section, we will see how effectively you can influence by the way in which you present products, creations and services to your clients.

5.5   Step 4: Presenting

As a reader of this book you certainly have learnt how to present a product, and notably the need to focus on the function and the services obtained, rather than only on the product's characteristics.

It is true that some sales advisors do present a product only by describing the product. There is definitely no point in doing this! There is no added value in just saying that the car is a car, red in color, with four wheels and that it is a 5-seater. Customers can see this. In the same way, there is no point in listing the car's characteristics to the customer. He can see that you are not bringing any added value and he could get this information by just reading the description panel himself. Or worse, he has already informed himself before coming and what the sales advisor says is akin to *déjà vu*.

A well-presented product will receive far fewer objections. We invite you to go further than simply talking about the benefits in a Luxury selling approach.

5.5.1 The Dimensions Of A Product

This consists of looking differently at what you sell in order to present it in a richer, more interesting, and in a much more effective light.

- Facts: what is the product and what superiority does it offer to customers?

"We have been engineering 4-wheel drive steering for over a hundred years and therefore we have all the necessary experience. You are acquiring a proven and superior technology."

- Functional benefits: what it brings to customers?

'The system will provide you with full security, especially in bad weather conditions—you know that unfortunately weather can be totally unpredictable, but your vehicle is ready no matter what happens."

- Emotional resonance: what emotions it elicits in customers?

"Our patented 4-wheel drive steering system is synonymous with security, and this also means responsibility, for you, as a driver."

- Pleasure: what pleasure the product can bring to the customer?

"The feeling of control is just amazing—you are only driving normally and yet you get that powerful road control sensation, it's just magic."

- Possible frustrations: what the customer might miss out on if he does not acquire the product?

"Imagine your car without 4-wheel drive steering and you are suddenly caught in a bad snow storm."

5.5.2 A Product Is an Addition of Decisional Components

Henry with John Hudson:

Henry:	"Mr. Hudson, here is your selection which I am sure you would like to review first. I know that you are already knowledgeable about all the technical aspects but please let tell you a little more. Our brand invented four-wheel power more than a century ago! Our engineering creators were already thinking not only about performance, but also about security."
Henry:	"This new design has been generously inspired by the spirit of exploration for comfortable, urban adventure, and more. Let me show you these very exciting new design additions."
Henry:	"We will also be very proud to have you joining us. We will be with you for a 2-year personal follow-up period, and I will personally take good care of your account."

Table 5.5.A Explaining benefits

Factors	Product Benefits	Customer Benefits	Sales Advisor
Brand	Luxury car image	Brand's image and quality assurance.	"Our Brand's image of quality and security is not by chance—you know that we deserve it and that's why you come to us."
Product	Premium	Will have the best.	"It's about driving pleasure but also the security of your dear family. It's your responsibility and here you have chosen the best."
Price	High-end	Sure of the excellence and exclusiveness.	"It's certainly not low but you know that excellence is costly…You can be sure that our price is only the reflection of superior quality, and exclusive services."
Service	Great service and possible long-term relationship	Will have great after sales service, personalized relationship.	"We pride ourselves in having many happy customers, satisfied by our high-end after sales service and personal relationship—this is something many others brands cannot provide."
Time	New, trendy	Will be the first, an opinion leader.	"This new model will certainly be noticed because it's the best on the market at the moment. And you will see many people, very jealous of this beauty!"

Henry: "This is a newly launched model! I will make sure that you will receive it within 7 weeks should you take the purchase decision today."

A product is not just an item, or a solution. Most of the time it's from a brand, with a very wide scope of technical features but also related services, purchased from a place or someone who is going to provide additional services, at a certain price and available at a certain moment.

Presenting only the product itself is not sufficient. By understanding the decisional factors, you can very effectively influence and progress more quickly toward a buying decision (Table 5.5.A).

5.5.3   A Product Is An Addition Of Intelligence

A high priced product is never expensive simply because of marketing. It certainly has elements to justify the price: it's a sum of intelligence, not only an accumulation of materials.

Henry: "Mr. Hudson, please sit in the driver's seat and let me adjust the best position for you. You'll see that not only are you comfortable but it's also very easy for you to read and access all the information, like a pilot. This has been carefully designed. It's simple, and simply intelligent."

You need to take time to explain the why. Why the driver's seat has been designed with this shape—what makes it particularly comfortable? There are many explanations waiting for an expert sales advisor to bring them to light. When you explain to your customer, he will understand the superiority of the features. When he sees another car, he will check if these features are there. When he sits again in the driver's seat, he feels all the comfort and understands why.

5.5.4   A Product Is Also A Creation

A product is high priced because it is rare and not easily produced. There is always creativity and the notion of a unique creation behind a rare product.

Let's imagine you are at an art gallery—better still, a modern art gallery. You see a very odd sculpture and you have no idea what it represents. The art specialist starts, not by telling you about the art piece itself, but about the artist. And tells you the "why": why only this artist is exceptional with his particular experience, vision and beliefs. The strange sculpture is the result, the fruit of this uniqueness. The art advisor also tells you how this sculpture relates to the other sculptures in general: it's a piece of art with a long history in the art of sculpting. He would of course also tell you what it represents and show you the extraordinary details and the highly skillful execution.

- An admirable creator

For the product you are selling, there must be a creator. Often, it's the brand's founder. He has a vision, values and explains the success of your company. Sometimes, if you look carefully at the past and dig through the different information you have, you might find that the creator of the company wanted to change the world and had an incredible ambition for himself, his company and also for mankind. The creator must be admirable.

> *Roger:* "Our institution's founders had always been, literally, obsessed by financial stability, having seen many important banks go into bankruptcy and thereby causing tremendous disasters for many families. Stability is our founder's key value and the reason you can trust our bank."

- With true creativity

There is no success without a hero, and certainly not without creativity. This creativity explains why your company is more successful than others. There must be an original idea, some way of thinking that was different from the others. Customers must understand that your products are different not from a marketing approach but owing to creativity. Marketing is rational: everyone and any brand can do it. It's different for creativity—which is always, unique, rare and very precious.

- A different vision

> *Lucy:* "Our *maison* creates and crafts to last! This is the true difference with high-end leather goods. Our design is timeless, material used are the best possible and the angled stitching, is not only nice—it's simply more solid. It's a handbag you will always be happy to carry."

You buy a product to use it, and an art piece to show it. The creation you present is not only for the here and now; customers should be able to project into the future. A creation is also a unique expression of taste, with shapes and colors. It's about personality, exclusivity and uniqueness.

> *Lucy*: "I hope that our choice of colors speaks to you. You know that we have a specific artistic approach and for sure, these colors are different and our customers are not shy; they know what they want."

Now that you see the product you are selling differently, we need to present it differently. Here is some advice in order to be able to succeed in this important phase of the selling process: if your customer does not like your product, he will object, or even worse, reject.

A Vineyard Story

Louis, owner of a very famous *château* in Bordeaux, welcomed me to his property. After warmly welcoming us, he invited me to see if the grapes were "behaving well today." It is of course impressive: all aligned, in perfect order. There aren't even any leaves on the soil. It was in June and we could just see the beautiful grapes forming. He looked at his grapes with love, and could not refrain from touching the leaves, as if he was caressing them. He explained that his family had owned this property for 60 years, and he was very happy to be able to continue to take care of it. "The soil," he said, "is the mother of all," and explained why the soil on his land is geologically special. He explained that it also differed thanks to generations of workers, experts that had been taking care of it, nourishing it and in return harvesting from Mother Soil the most beautiful grapes.
He walked me to the wine distillery, where we saw the huge stainless-steel containers. There was also a small laboratory. Everything was so clean and neat—exactly like the rows of grapes in the vineyard. At last he took me to the cellar, where he had prepared three bottles of wine from different years. "How do you like it?" Louis asked me. The wine I had had before the visit just tasted different.

5.5.5 Describe Elegantly

> *Henry*: "Mr. Hudson, you can see here the computerized dashboard. It's composed of two very user-friendly indicators—a speedometer and tachometer. It is simple and very easy to read. On the right side you can find a central computer, with an oversized screen. This will allow particularly clear and neat road guidance. It can also display all the information you may need, with touch control or even voice control."
>
> *Martial*: "Along with the dial, you can also see the 4 Roman numerals as indexes. These are slightly oversized—very generous. The numerals are visibly larger in size. They look like they were

hand-painted. And this gives a very nice balance between the off-white, vintage feel of the dial contrasting with this shiny, very dark inscription."

Lucy: "We use only the best calfskin as you can see here. Please feel the softness at the same time as the robustness of the premium leather our brand selected. In terms of lining, it's a printed silk-like extra-resistant and truly light material. The different metallic parts are all gold plated, superbly resistant with over 10 microns of plating. It is also very light as you can feel. This is obtained by a combination of different skills and research so as to answer to the criteria requested by active customers such as you!"

When you describe a product, be sure of these 3 important rules:

– Use simple, elegant words
– Show what you describe (gesture)
– Speak slowly

A description of the product should never be flat, and only factual. The words you choose, the way in which you speak and the way you handle the product are an extremely important part of the presentation.

Golden Rule Corner

You only like what you know, and you love what you understand. Be prepared to explain some key intelligent features of your product.

5.5.6 Showing It Is Better Than Saying It

Martial: "Mr. Wang, can I please I tell you more about the creation of the dial of this timepiece? As you can see, it's a white—more precisely, an off-white, that is very close to the traditional vintage ceramic dial color that you see in all antique pocket watches. Our creator wants to pay tribute to the grand tradition of watch making and insisted on incorporating this color as part of the design code. The subtle white looks like it has been aged, and gives this restful charm that you will probably not see in another white dial…It's not just painted—our workshop has developed and innovated a process to create a color that answers to our brand creator's demanding criteria."

Roger: "Please let me show you a simple graph. This is simply the growth of this financial vehicle over the last fifteen years. You can see that it's doing nicely, increasing steadily. This graph simply shows a very nice balance between growth and preservation of wealth for our clients. What you see here is what you can expect from us when everything is going smoothly."

Alice: "Sir, why don't you take this magnificent necklace and check the quality of the different stones our expert in-house gemologist has carefully selected? You can be sure that there is no possible compromise. Please, here is the *loupe* and you can start checking with the biggest stones: you will see, it's simply magnificent. Only the best possible diamonds deserved to be mounted here."

We tend to believe what we see, more than what any sales advisor tells us. This is simply because a client knows that a sales advisor is there to sell and, therefore, sometimes suspects that he would not always tell the whole truth and only the truth. On the other hand, customers almost always believe in their own judgment and what they can see with their own eyes.

By asking customers to look at something and experience it for themselves, you are proving the product's quality. It will appear authentic. The customer tends to think: "If a sales advisor dares to ask me to look and feel, it must be true."

Most of the time, visual impact is essential: customers remember images, pictures and graphs more than the spoken word. An iPad/tablet can display pictures but I also recommend that you include traditional printed materials, such as newspapers and magazine clippings (un-challengeable), and some official or corporate printed documents (in-house reports, industry news, indexes and so on), in your presentations. Customers assess information according to their personal credibility ranking and sometimes information on an iPad/tablet is not sufficient unless it has a certain cachet of authenticity.

5.5.7 Prove It, Since It's True

Henry: "Mr. Hudson, instead of telling more about the effectiveness of the 4-wheel drive system, please let me show you a very short video. Here we go…"

Roger: "Mr. Morgan, we are an institution. In our current portfolio, we have over 100,000 family accounts just like yours. We are one of the most solid banks in financial history, recognized by all professionals in this sector. You can feel 100% safe with us."

Martial: "Mr. Wang, here are some of the latest auction prices of our high-end timepieces. I have noted the initial prices and the last prices paid at auction. I made a very quick calculation based on this last auction where five of our brand's timepieces were proposed for sale. The average increase per year was over 15%. I believe it's significant and I want you to take this value increase into consideration."

Don't ask the customer to believe you: just prove to them that what you are saying is true.

5.5.8 Demonstrate The Simplicity

Alice: "Madame, please let me show you how to open the clasp on this necklace. It's actually very easy. First, please hold it with your left hand, and turn it this way. Then use the index finger of your right hand to block here and lift with your thumb this way. You see it's quite easy. And you don't need help from your husband even if I am sure that he would love to assist you!"

A live demonstration is the best way to deal with any usage questions. The idea is to take the time to do/show it, and at the same time clearly explain the steps (maximum 3 steps) while doing it. After a demonstration, customers tend to request trying the product for themselves. I suggest assisting the customer by slowly talking though each step and inviting the customer to take their time. There is always a risk that the customer does not manage to use the product on their first attempt and this will create doubt about the ease of operation.

5.5.9 Tell Stories About The Product

Henry: "I want also to share a story with you! Last year one of my clients called me to say that he felt so lucky. He was driving during winter and went off the road. He managed to control the car and avoided an accident. He called me the next day and wanted me to know."

Lucy: "Our designer really spent time looking at our archives. He was inspired by this design, which in fact has just as much to say today, and with such modernity. When it was presented, it immediately met great success—probably because it looks familiar to everyone and at the same time, so different from what you would have seen previously. That's exactly what our designer wanted!"

5.5.10 Focus On Main Selling Points

Another piece of advice is to be very clear about the main selling points. You don't need many and you certainly shouldn't present all the selling points at the same time. Customers only have enough attention to absorb 2 to 3 selling points at any one time. It's better to use this time to fully explain the prime selling points in order to sure they are absorbed. Since they are important, these selling points should not be wasted. I even recommend expert sales advisors to write out these selling points in the way they want to talk about them, adding stories to raise interest.

How-to Corner

For each product, list the 3 main selling points, called prime points. You can add further selling points later, but in general this should be enough!

5.5.11 Handle With Care: It's Precious

The way products are handled lends importance and status to them. For watches and jewelry, the wearing of gloves is not only to protect and avoid micro-scratches (fingers do damage) but also to show that these pieces are precious and need to be handled with respect and care.

Before handing a product to a customer, be sure to first check whether the product is in perfect condition. If need be, clean it (for example, the handle of a car, the sapphire crystal glass of a watch and so on). Look at your product. Take the time to check it in front of your customer—you will demonstrate how precious the product is, and how important your customer is.

All gestures have to be elegant. The way in which a sales advisor handles a watch, a piece of jewelry or a handbag shows not only the professionalism but the quality of the products presented. Even with a financial leaflet, it has to be crisp, brand new and, ideally, stored in a protective folder. The leaflet is new—it is only for your customer. There is a need for some *mise en scène*: your product needs to be on stage, and deserves the full limelight.

When presenting a product, remember the 2-R rule: romance and reassure

5.5.12 Romance and Reassure

Romancing is the story about the product and around the product. It's the best way to capture attention, create interest and provoke desire.

Reassurance is to prove that the product is the safe choice. It's the best way to reduce possible objections, create perceived value, and diminish the customer's fears.

5.6   Step 5: Convincing

With good preparation, you are ready for the selling stage. After a very nice, warm and efficient welcoming, you managed to get the customer's attention and they have agreed to spend time with you. After a phase of discovering the customer's desires you have an idea of what to propose—linking the customer with what you have in your portfolio to sell. You present with flair, create desire, and, at the same time, reassure.

If everything goes well, you would probably have covered 70–80% of the selling process and created an irresistible desire in the customer to purchase. But still, things are not always easy. You are selling a high-end product, with a high price tag and with a significant decision making process.

5.6.1   Detect The Level Of Interest

During the presentation, the signs of interest are multiple and they are not difficult to perceive:

- *Customer focuses on one product*

When a customer starts to focus on one product or one offer: the customer stops browsing and selects a product for consideration

- *Customer is available, relaxed*

When the customer exhibits a relaxed mood, and is open to listening further: the customer will feel that it's worth spending time with you.

- Customer questions

The customer starts to ask questions about the brand and products, and shows a strong interest

- Customer speaks about himself

This is a way for your customer to establish a good relationship: and it allows the sales advisor to be more precise in their advice

- Customer asks for more choices

Often seen as a lack of interest, a customer request is in fact a sign of buying interest. Why would a customer spend time considering more choices if he or she has no intention of buying?

- Customer inquiress about the price

As discussed, it is always advisable not to mention the price unless asked. Price is not the principal reason for buying! And, a customer who asks for the price is already showing a first sign of his willingness to purchase.

- Customer offers general reasons for not buying

In my experience, at some point in the conversation many customers have a tendency to mention general reasons for not buying as way to protect themselves from buying. It may be that the general economy is not good or it is not the right time to spend money. Customers may mention that they have already spent a lot recently and should be careful. All these general reasons reveal buying interest but indicate that the timing is not absolutely right and yet they are not truly objecting.

The most important signs of buying are the objections. But before understanding this, you need to be fully aware of the importance of fear.

5.6.2 Fear: A Powerful and Normal Sentiment

As we have seen at the beginning of the selling journey, the key difference between a professional buyer and a customer is the capacity (I should say necessity) to define their purchase specifications. Luxury-seeking customers do not shop professionally. Their desires have to be clarified with the assistance of the sales advisor.

The reasons for not buying are always linked to fear. Such fear is very much anchored deeply in our soul, body and behavior. Fear is good: it is part of our survival instinct. It also dictates our social experience: how we are raised in the family environment and our educational environment.

- Fear of making a mistake

> *Peter:*   "It's a new brand: you can never be sure about the future. I am really not sure if I shall commit to a new brand like yours."

The main reason for this is the fear of making a mistake. And this fear is deeply and fundamentally entrenched: parents ask children to do the right thing—and bring in needed adjustments where necessary. And teachers are there to prevent children from making too many mistakes, and correct them when needed.

- Fear of disappointment

> *Mr. Taylor:*   "I want to be sure that my wife will not regret this choice."

The fear of disappointment is also related to the fear of making a mistake but with a social dimension. If I made a mistake that impacts me, it's less important than a wrong decision that will impact my family and friends.

- Fear that it is "not worth it"

> *Lisa:*   "For this price, I am pretty sure I can find a similar bag at a top prestigious brand!"

This is the financial dimension of the fear. We are all educated and well versed in trading, exchanging. In the school playground we exchanged our possessions against another things, and each time, it had to be worth it. This sentiment is strong. The "worth it or not" feeling is far from being rational; it's a sentiment that can paralyze.

Table 5.6.A Customers' fears

	Fear	Objection From Lisa
Brand	Wrong brand	"To tell you the truth, I am not at all sure about your brand."
Product	Wrong choice	"Well, it's not exactly what I am looking for."
Price	Too expensive	"Your price looks very high, unless there is a promotional offer?"
Place	Wrong location, wrong sales advisor	"I might buy it in Milan, because I often go there."
Time	Too early	"It's not very urgent, I can wait."

- Fear of guilt

> *John:* "I am not sure—you know, maybe I should select a more entry-level option. We still have children with over 10 years of educational needs to pay for!"

Guilt is a generous sentiment. Customers might feel guilty for spending a large amount of money on themselves.

These fears also exist at the 5 decision making motivational factors level and can seriously impact the decision making process (Table 5.6.A):

It is essential that you are able to classify all objections into these 5 fear categories, in order to deal efficiently with the different techniques that we propose.

5.6.3 Objection, Expression Of Fears

> *Peter:* "Let me be very clear with you: I just want to know more but please understand that there is no chance I will buy such a new brand."
>
> *Martial:* "I understand, Sir, and it is already a privilege for me to be able to present our brand to you. I am not sure that our brand can be considered as so new, with already 20 years of existence, and, most importantly, total recognition from the industry as being one of the most traditional, respected brands in true watchmaking heritage."

Let's be very happy and positive about all the possible objections. It's because your customer has the intention to purchase that your customer tells you why he or she is not willing to buy. What if the customer simply walked away without telling the sales advisor anything, purely and simply to escape? The objections are at the center of the success: it's a real and important conversational opportunity that is not to be missed.

- An objection is not always nice to hear.

> *Lisa*:   "You must be dumb to buy here when you know that it's far more expensive than in Europe!"

An objection is an immediate expression of a fear, and therefore could be brutal and not always very nice to hear. You still have to keep a very positive mindset and see the positive side. Notably by changing customer's remark into a nice question in your mind: "I don't want to look stupid by buying here when everyone knows that it's much cheaper to buy in Italy, where the handbag is produced. Could you please tell me, dear sales advisor, why I should buy here please?"

This is the perfect opportunity for any sales advisor to explain why the customer should buy now!

- An objection is sometimes violent, and it may seem like there is no answer.

> *Lisa*:   "I cannot buy it unless you give me 20% off. Just take it or leave it."

Again, because you are a qualified sales advisor, do not consider an objection to be anything more than a question. There could be an element of negotiation in the remark, as is the case in Lisa's remark above—but it is still fundamentally a question, formulated in a hurry and under the emotional stress of having to make a decision.

> *Lucy*:   "I would be delighted to offer you a welcoming accommodation if it were possible. And, I know that some brands do mark up prices and afterwards offer discounts so as to please customers. Ultimately, it's a practice that does not help customers. We prefer to have fair pricing from the beginning with the objective of giving customers full confidence in our prices, worldwide."

Take the objection positively, and again, turn it into a question: "Dear sales advisor, I don't think that your price is fair and I believe that there is a possibility for you to offer me 20% so as to make me feel fully comfortable with my purchase. If you don't, I will not feel reassured and therefore cannot take my decision."

- An objection is sometimes unclear.

> *Lisa*:   "I don't know why, but I just feel that this is not right."

It's absolutely normal to receive an unclear objection. Handling such objections is part of the expert sales advisor's job description: helping a customer to clarify their desire, but also fears. The same rule applies: turn the objection into a question: "I still don't feel comfortable enough to buy and suspect something is wrong. I don't know exactly what, but there is still some worry at my level. Could you please assist me in understanding my hesitation?"

There are a few techniques to clarify these objections:

- ● ***Invitation to clarify***

> *Lisa*:   "Clearly, if you are still hesitating, it means that there is still an uncomfortable zone and thank you for telling me this. I can see that you love this handbag. Could it be some others factor which is causing you to hesitate such as our brand or the price?"

Express that you see the hesitation but do not understand why. This approach sometimes helps the customer to realize that actually there is nothing to worry about.

- ● ***"Imagining the consequences" question***

> *Lucy*:   "Let me help you on this. Imagine you had decided to purchase this. What could be the possible regrets?"
>
> *Lisa*:   "Looking at it this way, I guess I'm not very sure about the color."
>
> *Lucy*:   "I know that you were hesitating about this fuchsia bag and you were thinking more about opting for red. I am not sure it would be as nice in red as it is in this very sharp, vibrant fuchsia. And, I'm not sure if it will go very well with your style. While this beautiful, trendy and modern fuchsia suits you particularly well—on this, I am sure. I am

certain you will not regret the choice of this lively fuchsia. It's the right one given that this model is from our brand."

Lisa: "You are right."

Most of the time the consequences of a decision are exaggerated in the mind of the customer. By imagining the possible consequences, customers might discover that, in fact, there is much less to worry about than they might imagine.

- An objection can be hidden.

The objection is very often hidden, or more exactly not expressed clearly enough. The most terrible one to hear is certainly: "Thank you, I will think about it." This is often understood to be a "no." It should firstly be interpreted as a timing objection: "Dear advisor, I consider that it's clear enough on my side. But I will need more time to think about taking the decision."

Michelle Taylor: "Thank you, that was quite an experience. We've just arrived in Paris and we do want to visit other nice boutiques." (Here there is a hidden objection to the brand.)

Alice: "It's a great pleasure to have met you and I am glad to have helped you find this beautiful necklace; it's perfect for you and your husband's wedding anniversary. I understand that you would like to take more time and browse other brands. We are extremely proud to be one of the very 'happy few' major jewelry *maisons* in Paris. I am not sure that there are many others that you will be able to compare with our *maison*!"

- An objection can be just emotional.

Paul Morgan: "Frankly speaking, but please don't take it badly, I just don't trust you or any financial institution. That is why I did not subscribe to any of the life insurance or long-term savings plans, or whatever you call it."

It can happen that customers just throw out their emotional concerns and require reassurance. It is of course never personal. The customer is not over-reacting: again it's an expression of a certain fear, and a particular way of asking a question: "Dear sales advisor, I don't trust you because you represent financial institutions which I don't trust. So don't blame me for that. Can you tell me why I should trust you when I don't trust any financial institution?"

Roger can also answer with empathy and a personal touch:

> *Roger*: "Mr. Mason, I understand your position regarding financial institutions and you know you are not the only one who distrusts them after the many bankruptcies and lack of ethical standards that everyone has heard about on the news. I am not here to defend my industry but I do want to invite you to see my bank as an individual company, doing its very best, and I am, as an honest and humble person, here to help you to find the best financial solutions."

Golden Rule Corner

An objection is an expression of fear. You have to see it as a question, which is calling for an answer: reassurance.

- Terrible time objection.

> *John Hudson*: "Okay, that was quite a good conversation. Give me more time to think about it."

Most sales advisors hear this objection and don't even think of it as an objection. It should be understood as: "I've had enough for today but I am still not ready to take a decision. I don't want to make a mistake and I am not sure that if I decide to purchase, it will be risk-free. I don't see why I should decide now. Can you tell me?"

> *Henry Smith*: "Thank you and I can see that you really like the car you carefully selected. I can see that you are a wise person. Why not decide today?"

5.6.4 Dealing With Objections

Since an objection is only an expression of fear, it also serves as a special type of question that customers tend to ask before taking a decision. This is a crucial phase. It could be tense: a customer might show signs of self-defense, a very normal and legitimate behavior. Something must be wrong: it could not be so pleasant and easy otherwise. The expression of this fear is positive as we have discussed but it is not always delivered in a positive, friendly manner. It depends on the customer's personality and on the situation. Let's start with the general attitude and the 3-step innovative approach I propose.

Step 1: Truly accept

Show that you recognize the client's legitimacy in putting forward the objection.
"You are right Lisa to carefully consider the color."

Also, thank her for engaging in a conversation about her fear, and what makes her hesitate.
"Thank you Lisa for telling me how you feel about the color."

Show that you understand the importance of the objection for the client.
"I understand, the choice of the color is crucial to your decision."

Show that you are available for that conversation: it is a very interesting subject.
"Sure, and please let me tell you about the palette of colors offered…"

The right non-verbal behavior would be to continue to smile without any change in your attitude. Because you accept the objection doesn't mean that you agree with it. It's an encouragement to the customer to tell you more, and at the same time it's a recognition that the customer really does want to buy.

Avoid giving the impression that you have met with this kind of objection a thousand times before. Take a few seconds before you deal with the objection: you will show that you have taken time to think and consider your answer before you strike back.

Step 2: Deal smoothly

> *Lucy*: "If this handbag was in red, maybe it would not look as nice as the one here in fuchsia—it's the right balance between the color, the shape and all the detailing. And, maybe you will not like it as much as the one

you have here? I am just trying to figure out what it would look like, if
it was in red."

Lucy: "Perhaps it's because you came with the idea of finding a red handbag.
Why not forget about that idea for the moment and let the fuchsia
color sit with you to see how you feel?"

Lucy: "It seems to me that the most important thing is that you like what
have in hand right now because here, you know whether you like it or
not…I would forget about the possible red color."

Given the importance of the subject, I will list hereafter the key techniques
for influencing. For now, let's focus on the principle, on the persuasive
approach. And let's do some math, considering:

O as the customer's Objection,
P as your Proposal
T the Truth

And this creates a paradox at the level of the customer's mindset:
O is what I think T is.
P is what the sales advisor wants me to believe.

If P is too different from O, it means that P is not T.

In fact, the truth is somehow unknown (…and that's why I am asking).

The key and most important finding is that the customer only has to resolve
the equation of what T is—the truth. And most likely the truth is $T = O + P$.

The only correct approach is to politely put forward the proposal to counterbalance O and create a truth seeking dynamic. There are various ways in
which we can deliver the proposal and we will review extensively the
techniques for influencing.

But, remember, the most important aspect is to counterbalance the O.
You don't need to prove that $P = T$.

Avoid creating doubts about the fact that:
$O = T$ might not be true, and that
$P = T$ might be possible.

Step 3: Close nicely

Back to Lisa:

> *Lucy:*   "But you are right to consider which is the best color for your style. I think red might be good, but with this fuchsia you just look amazing! By the way, we also have a small wallet in the same color which goes with the handbag."

Back to Paul Morgan:

> *Roger:*   "Of course you are right to be cautious and that's why we took the necessary time to discuss the company's values. I propose that I walk you through all the different charges that might occur during your investment period—we aim to be fully transparent and give you all the necessary information before you make your decision. You don't need to worry about us. By the way, not all banks are bad and it's just that some are particularly damaging, I suppose like all industries right?"

After dealing smoothly with objection, it's time to give the power back to the customer, so as to re-establish the balance. It's time to compliment, to measure the progress and to lead on to another subject. Customers should not perceive your proposal as right and his objection as wrong. You are simply proposing a different way to approach the purchase, a different perspective.

The different techniques for dealing with objection

- Offer concrete facts to counteract uncertain feelings.

When Peter, as seen previously, was unsure about the brand he was looking at, the sales advisor came forward with hard facts. These facts are solid and concrete: precise numbers, remarks that cannot be challenged, pictures, videos, quotes and so on.

- Tell a true story.

Let's go back to the situation of Michelle Taylor's brand objection:

Alice: "Madame, I also recently heard a nice story which I would like to tell you. A customer from London really loved her choice but wanted to check additional brands and I even gave her few recommendations for brands she could consider who are at our level. She looked at the list and just told me 'okay, I am ready to purchase'. She avoided wasting time because the others brands were not inspiring enough for her."

- Create doubt upon objection.

And let's see with Peter:

Peter: "Maybe, but your brand is a baby compared to brands that have a hundred or even two hundred years of history."

Martial: "I understand and hope you will allow me one remark, Sir. Many brands have over one century of history and you just don't even want to look at their products. Would you prefer to have a brand with a history but no true value or quality, or another younger brand which does offer true value and quality?"

Peter: "The best brands, of course, have both heritage and true watch-making expertise."

Martial: "You are absolutely right but there are not that many of them as you know. Our proposal to collectors is to acquire a history of the future! We are very confident about our extraordinary watchmaking expertise. And that expertise can only be spotted by a true collector like you!"

The objective is simply to create doubt. Peter will think: *"Maybe I should not buy from only those brands with over a hundred years of history, because it's true that some are not good. A 100-year existence should not be the only criteria. Watchmaking expertise is more important. So maybe the younger brand is still an option, if I am convinced."Note to the publisher - I was unable to modify the italics to straight lettering!!!*

- Leave the objection for later.

Martial: "Allow me first to tell you more about this new mechanical move-ment that our creator has just invented."

Peter: "We are talking about your brand. You are changing the subject right?"

Martial: "It's actually the same. I'd like to show you what our brand is about in concrete terms. I believe that will ease any apprehension."

Peter: "So, this is something new or an adaptation?"

Martial: "Well, it's fully innovative as you can see yourself."

It's sometimes necessary to postpone the answer with these possible benefits:

- The objection is not so important and the customer accepts your answer
- The objection is resolved naturally with time (better understanding)
- The objection is not clear and cannot be answered clearly
- The objection is particularly unfair and therefore leaving it aside is a sign of tact, if not training
- The objection has already been answered and it is a better use of time to move on

5.6.5 Price Objection

Price objection appears as the main closing obstacle though it is not especially different from the other objections. I would say that often times it's an even smaller objection since there is ground for finding a common understanding. Unlike size, color and other subjective, taste and purely emotional preferences, price is pretty factual. You need to understand what the objection is to a price and the fears related to it.

• **Understanding prices**

A high value product does not mean it is expensive to your affluent customer. If they are looking, it most likely means that they can afford it. The level of price is simply related to the quality and the category of the product. The perception of price largely depends on the wealth of your customer.

And a product in itself is never too "expensive." Again, affluent customers are used to buying high value products. A car costing a million US$ can be seen as reasonable when it is perceived as having a great value. It is expensive only when it is perceived to have no inherent value. If it could be seen as having less value than the price reflects, then it isn't worth it. Customers compare products they know and use their former experience. Most of the time, they simply suspect that the price is artificially set, and set far too high (Table 5.6.B).

What you need to do is to be able to explain a price and defend it.

Table 5.6.B Explaining the price

	Possible Themes	Car Example
Brand	Legitimacy, image, heritage, exclusivity.	"As you might know, our brand is not only a brand—we symbolize quality and security."
+ Product	Quality, cost to produce, rarity, durability.	"All brands claim security is important—we are really making it more secure, better than all other systems available in cars on the market."
+ Place	Service, after sales service, customer care.	"Because our focus is on your experience, we also care about the after sales service. We offer an incomparable list of extra services that we are the only ones to offer."
+ Time	Newness, opportunity, time savings, pleasure of the moment.	"This model is new and you will be the first to enjoy all the technology and awesome design."
= Price	Fair/correct/best price, investment, return on purchase value.	"It's definitely a Luxury car and you deserve it! And if you take the time to do the math, you will see that it's a very good return on investment."

- A price is a sum of values

The best way to explain the value of your price is to do some math:
Brand
+ Product
+ Place
+ Time
= Price

- A price is an investment

Martial: "Mr. Wang, you are a successful businessman and I am sure that you can also see in this timepiece, collectible value and investment opportunity."

Peter: "I am not sure how this will increase. While with some traditional brands, the increase has been proven, right?"

Martial: "Precisely, Sir. The magic part is the unknown! The true collectors are the ones able to find the treasure before anyone else."

Peter: "The risk is higher with new brands—to have bet on the wrong horse!"

> *Martial*:   "Sir, I am sure that you always invest wisely. With our time-pieces—with the quality and rarity we offer—I think we can be sure that they will not lose value. Now the question is by how much can it increase?"

Luxury creations and high value products are rare most of the time and prices do increase every year. Raw materials and skilled labor costs increase very quickly, every year. There is also a market for reselling to collectors. You need to present the following two considerations to the customers: buying today is cheaper and the product will be worth much in the future.

- A price is profitable

A Luxury creation is of a higher quality and therefore is built to last. A very good handbag could last a lifetime. A piece of jewelry or a collectible timepiece can also be handed down to the next generation. When you look at what you have bought, generally speaking, it is most likely the case that the low-priced products you purchased have been damaged or lost. You look after the high value items more carefully simply because they are of a superior quality and they are intended to last. A good pair of shoes can last years, and stay smart. A good and reliable car saves time, even lives. In many cases, depending on the product, it is always possible to find examples that demonstrate that quality can also mean savings for those who can afford the initial purchase.

Simon Cole convinced Sophie and Thomas Williams on the price of the house:

> *Thomas*:   "The price of this house is far from our initial budget and you know that."
>
> *Simon*:   "Is there any risk that you don't like it?"
>
> *Sophie*:   "I think we are safe on that side—it's the perfect family townhouse."
>
> *Simon*:   "Okay, that's very valuable you know. It means that you don't take the risk of moving out—which always represents a high cost. And if you choose to keep it for many years, you are pretty much guaranteed that the house's value will increase nicely."
>
> *Thomas*:   "But we will still to have to invest more."
>
> *Simon*:   "Yes, you are right. As far as your investment will be profitable in terms of cost saving and potential gains in the future, I believe it's worth considering. My job as advisor is to present you with all the options from a profitability perspective, and encourage you to view price from different angles."

- A price is a saving

Prices do increase and this is especially the case with luxury and high value items. They are rare and complex to produce and require many components that are rare, expensive and, therefore, come with the high possibility of price increases in the future.

Allan Taylor:	"I can see that my wife likes this necklace. Now I am not sure that the price is the right one to be very frank with you."
Alice:	"Yes, it's almost as if it was specially designed for Michelle! About the pricing of such a beautiful piece of jewelry, we are a highly reputed jewelry house because, of course, for a long time now we have ensured all our creations are fairly priced and have created a fair pricing policy. It takes into account the gold, diamonds and so on but also the workmanship and time."
Allan:	"Do you mark down the prices of old pieces?"
Alice:	"Oh, very often it's the contrary. You know that prices for diamonds and gold are always on the increase. Prices therefore will continue to increase. Not taking into account the salary of the various artisans who can work over a hundred or even a thousand hours on the collections. These labor costs in rare craftsmanship also increase very rapidly. To make it short, buying today might already offer a saving since prices increase all the time."

The argument that buying today is cheaper than buying tomorrow is a recognized and very often true fact. If possible, you can even calculate the average increase and show examples through different catalogs if need be.

- *Price is also pride (no italics!)*

Allan Taylor:	"Still, there are quite some digits in the price tag!"
Alice:	"Absolutely, Sir, and it's definitely an important art piece that not many people can afford! Mrs. Taylor can be very proud of your decision!"

Customers do not only want to own, invest and save. A high price also symbolizes power. There is nothing wrong in the desire to feel powerful. It's very often an attribute of affluent customers without there being any arrogance, it is simply the result of a feeling of achievement and reward. Why not encourage customers to think in this way?

* **Understanding Fears On Prices**

- Fear of overpricing

Allan Taylor, like anyone else, wants to be sure that he is not overpaying. For a Luxury creation and high price product, the price is pretty difficult to compare. A necklace's price is not a sum of the number of diamonds. For a sports car, how can you compare it with another model? Normally a Marketing Department has done a great job and price is fairly defined.

Weaker sales advisors tend to question their own brand's prices while the more experienced sales advisors focus on how to defend and explain the prices.

John Hudson:	"I feel that the price for the same category of car is very high!"
Henry Smith:	"Not sure with what you would compare Mr. Hudson."
John:	"For a SUV, 4-wheel drive"
Henry:	"It's pretty large segment, Sir. We are definitely premium—that's the only way we can deliver the best quality. There is a huge team of market researchers in our company and I trust that we are absolutely within the market price. Besides, we are, and I repeat, again very focused—if not only focused—on security which means quality. We cannot go low and therefore compromise. Security is about life and it is priceless."

Golden Rule Corner

Defending a price is first about believing in the price and being able to explain it and defend it. Don't be weak—trust your price.

Fear Of Going Over Budget

The Williams were afraid of going over budget:

Thomas:	"I am also not very sure if we can afford the mortgage."
Simon:	"Well on this side, if you need my help I can help you to estimate. But I guess that this is something pretty personal."
Thomas:	"You are right. I roughly calculated about an increase of 25% compared to what we were prepared to spend per month."
Simon:	"May I share with you my experience on this? This situation happens all the time. The most important consideration is not the initial budget you set per month. But considering the house

and its new budget per month, would this be something you are willing to invest?"

Thomas: "It's true that with 25% per month it's still affordable even we have to be a little bit more cautious."

Simon: "Well, your mortgage is not lost right? It's an investment in the long run,
Thomas. From this angle for sure it looks better."

Most of the time, the notion of budget is not the main lock. The most important factor is to relate the cost to the income or wealth. In doing so, the cost then seems smaller and suddenly affordable.

- Fear of overpaying

No one wants to pay more than others and that, of course, includes your affluent customers. Being wealthy does not mean that you don't consider cost. You certainly hate the idea of overpaying just like anyone else.

Moreover, affluent customers buy and trade more than most people and are familiar with the buying process. They love the idea of acquiring at the best price.

5.6.6 Facing Bargaining

Despite offering an explanation and price justification, it is not always possible to successfully close the price conversation. Customers may persist in asking for a lower price. Customers are also encouraged to do this by the fact that, very often, brands and retailers do offer price accommodations. These price accommodations are possibly to:

— Compensate for pricing differences between different markets
— Sell some products faster (former collections, overstock)
— Match local customers' buying habits (when a certain level of discount is the norm)
— Facilitate closing the sale

Since prices might be not fixed—accommodations exist. It is normal that customers ask for, and will do their best to obtain, the best price. Of course, the best approach by brands would be a no-discount policy, which many brands and retailers are indeed implementing. The right attitude when facing

Table 5.6.C Defending the different prices

Desire	Customer's State Of Mind	Bargaining
Real price	The price published is not real	"I can buy cheaper in others countries or in another place anyway"
Fair price	The price is too high compared to the product's value	"I will not buy at this price; it's far too high for what it is—no way"
Good price for me	I need a special gesture	"I will not buy at this price for sure. What can you do for me?"
Best price only for me	I want the best possible price	"I'm not interested in your company's policy or whatever. You need to give me the best price you can. Ask your boss"

a price reduction request is to understand that your customer is right in asking—since this accommodation exists everywhere. And, rest assured, if your customer did not want to buy, he would not bargain (Table 5.6.C). You are very close to the decision being taken!

Four situations depend on the customer's desires in terms of price:

- A real price
- A fair price
- A good price for me
- A best price only for me

- Real price

In order to reassure a customer on price reality, you can prove the value by being particularly transparent in explaining pricing. Be aware of the prices offered in different countries and the practices of other retailers. Customers may have the impression that they can get lower prices somewhere else, from someone else.

John: "By the way, I just have to check at an independent car dealer and I am sure that I can order at a much lower price!"

Henry: "I am not sure which car dealer you are thinking about. Only three independent car retailers offer this model along with our brand's direct sales showroom. We know that sometimes commercial practices might differ slightly, but it would never be as important as you might think."

John: "But still, they can be cheaper than you right?"

Henry: "I really cannot say that. You need to compare the entire offer and the global package. We commit to deliver to you on time and very quickly. As I mentioned, I obtained important free options for you that my Management does not always offer to other customers. I really believe that we must have you as our client, and that you can even bring us more high-profile customers like you."

John: "I am sure that a car dealer will also be very happy to offer me free options. Everyone does it."

Henry: "John, if some car dealers can offer so much why would our show-room still exist? Actually, we are doing very, very well. I often have customers taking time to check all the possible distributors, show-rooms and come back to my offer. When the price is the same, what you really need to care about is the reliability, the service. Again, I can reassure you that if you have any possible questions, you can just give me a call and I will take care of it personally."

- Fair price

Customers believe that it is possible to ask for a price decrease because the product value isn't worth the price published. The best way to defend fairness in pricing is to not open the door to this discussion in the first place.

Let's get back to Lisa's price objection:

Lisa: "For this price, I am pretty sure I can find similar bags at top prestigious brands."

Lucy: "But maybe not as exciting as the one which is on your shoulder now."

Lisa: "I mean that the price seems too high compared to what it is else-where. I would say that the price is at least 30% higher than it should be, compared to other brands."

Lucy: "I understand that you need more confidence in our brand. We are one of the most prestigious leather goods *Maisons* and our prices reflect the brand value and the extraordinary quality. Our prices are not only true, and established with a consistent price policy world-wide, but also fair—totally reflecting the commitment and the quality behind each creation. Please be fully reassured on our pricing."

- Good price

Some customers will look for a "good price"—a price that is more advanta-geous compared to the "fair price." The customer wants an improvement; it could be an additional gift or some price accommodation. He wants to feel it is a good buy. Customers want to make sure they can benefit from promo-tions, and not miss a possible opportunity in the purchase.

Table 5.6.D Responding to price bargaining

	Customer	Response Angle
Fair Price	I am a fair person	"Sir, this is fair and you are not paying more than anyone else"
Good Price	I am a reasonable person	"Madame, this is a very good offer and you can be very happy with it"
Best Price	I am a champion	"Sir, we have already offered you the very best that we can offer. No one can get a better price than you"

- Best price

they can. Other customers will be "sportier"; they want to be sure to get the best price. Good is not enough; they want to be sure that no one can get a better price than they can. They might be business people or VIP clients of other brands. For them, negotiating is part of daily life and they negotiate sharply (Table 5.6.D).

5.6.7 Time To Summarize

Objections

An objection leads to a decision.
An objection is positive: it's only the expression of a fear.
An objection is no more than a question.
An objection is only an expression of the customer's point of view.

Dealing With Objections

In 3 steps: genuinely accept, deal smoothly with the objection and close politely.
There is no right or wrong, only different points of view.
Balance the customer's objection with your own position/proposal.
Creating doubt in the customer's mind is good enough.

5.7 Step 6: Closing

After following the advice in the lengthy section on convincing the customer, you might already have your customer on board, smoothly. We now have to detect the buying signs. In many cases, the sales advisor needs to offer a final helping hand to the customer so he can leave his fears aside once and for all, focus only the desire, and get fully motivated to make the purchase. And, experience shows that rare are the customers who bring out their credit card without being invited to do so.

5.7.1 Detect The Buying Signs

Sometimes, at this phase, customers may avoid the final purchase as a method of self-protection to avoid a possible buying mistake, as discussed. The most efficient way to detect this behavior is to open your eyes and ears and pick up on what is going on "behind the scenes." An astute sales advisor is able to quickly detect these signs and proceed elegantly to closing the sale.

- Changes in behavior

Even if one can hide behind words, it's much more difficult to hide one's emotions. Behavior always betrays us. For the sales advisor who is able to detect a change, and make an appropriate interpretation, the selling approach can be adapted to fit the moment. The first noticeable change is often a change in interest toward the sales advisor. Before taking a buying decision, customers do not really care about the sales advisor. But if the customer is to buy he needs to be sure to be able to trust, and benefit from, the service of the sales advisor. Customers ask more personal questions or pay more attention to sales advisors who are sending them warm, friendly and positive signals. Globally, all changes in behavior are expressions of a certain type of energy emitted in parallel to the deep consideration a customer is undertaking.

* Sudden attention to the sales advisor's brand
* Sitting up, a change in sitting position and crossing their legs
* Standing up or walking around
* Speed of talking—from normal to a slower or faster pace
* Commenting about the product, the brand

- Tension means decision

These tensions can be pretty vivid. It's an important decision and customers do not want to regret it. The sales advisor has been presenting the offer and explaining elegantly; the customer understands that they are expected to give an answer. Sales advisors are also feeling the tension, are under pressure and have a fear of losing the sale. Some customers tend to be more aggressive in challenging the sales advisor for the last time. Others might just be silent, going through the "pros" and "cons" in their head.

- Looking at the product from different angles or positions
- Trying the product again—touching
- Looking at the product description in detail

- Projection into the future

Everything concerning customer care, which is often only discussed after the purchase, may be brought up before the purchase in the form of cautious inquiries. The after sales service doesn't matter if you don't buy the product. This approach can pre-empt customers' concerns about:

- Solidity, durability
- Maintenance
- Precise details about security
- The after sales service
- The possibility of returning the product, or exchanging it

5.7.2 Focus On The Customer's Motivation

We are in persuasion mode at this stage. Remember, the customer is the one who takes the decision and, therefore, in this final stage of the decision making process, you need to deftly link the customer to his motivations.

Let's close with John Hudson and his car (Table 5.7.A).

By linking the five decision making motivational factors, you are very effectively consolidating the decision making by creating a very powerful sentiment: the decision is obvious.

Closing

Closing is to create the feeling that the decision to purchase is obvious.

Table 5.7.A Closing with the decision making motivational factors

Category	Sales Advisor	Closing Sentences
Brand	Our brand is you	"Paul, now that we have had this conversation, I don't picture you driving another brand other than ours"
Product	You made the right choice	"You love this model so much and, frankly speaking, it's perfect given the color and the options you've selected. It's very you"
Price	You obtained the best price	"You know that I already obtained for you more than I usually do and you really have the best possible price offer. You did really well in your negotiation"
Place	You are in the right place	"I will be your personal contact, you don't need to worry about anything. You came to me and I will make sure I work to deserve all your trust Paul"
Time	You are here at the right time	"You really came at the right time. We just launched and ordering now is the perfect timing for an early delivery to you"

Create A Decision Making Mood

- Feeling wise

Roger: "Mr. Morgan, you are impressive. All the questions you have asked are sensible and considered. We went through all the possible options to find the best plan for you. The best decision looks like a 15-year plan, with the first 7 years with a dynamic target and the remaining 8 years focusing on asset protection."

Paul: "Yes, this looks okay."

Roger: "There is no other better option and you really are making the right decision. I am so happy that we found it. Now this plan looks obvious because it is sensible and fully adapted to your personal situation."

Paul: "Maybe I shall sleep on it and we can finalize in another meeting?"

Roger: "John, let me just ask you a question: do you think that you will be able to find a better option than the one we just decided on? Personally, I don't think so. Even if some banks can propose something similar to our offer, they don't offer the credentials and the serious track record that we proudly have. It's the right decision, John. You could wait, but we both agree that this is the best offer and a sensible decision."

Roger: "You are making the right decision. Let me print the contract for you so you can re-read it and take more time to check all details."

The customer wants a sensible decision—a decision where the options have been carefully considered. One of the factors this customer is taking into account is the mistake of impulse buying. Even though there is always an element of impulse, it's essential to encourage the customer to see the sensible side of the decision process, and that the decision is a rational one.

- Feeling like a winner

Customers will buy if they feel that it is the correct decision: I am not only making a wise decision, my decision is one that comes from someone who has fought for it, and won. This feeling will create satisfaction and comfort for your customer.

Martial:	"Mr. Wang, you told me that you made some very good acquisitions in the past and I am very impressed. I am sure that because you are a winner you are able to detect winning creations."
Peter:	"I do have discerning eyes for the right and best watches. And, this time, my instinct told me to be careful about new brands, but at the same time, I have to say that I am quite seduced."
Martial:	"Trust your winner's instinct! Your feeling is right. You know, that's how all the best decisions are made."
Peter:	"Let's do this, Mr. Wang. Because it is our pride to have you come to our brand for the first time, and with this exceptional timepiece, I now commit that I will write to our founder's office to introduce you and ask for a special letter to thank you, signed by our founder. This is a special service that we normally only grant to our best customers. I will make sure that this will be approved."
Peter:	"That's very nice of you."
	"Let me now show you the beautiful mahogany box that will protect your watch. Thank you for your decision. It's such a nice moment."

A purchase must be a victory. It's a win. Customers must feel that something has been won and there are reasons for changing their mind. It's good to focus on a customer's win and express the exceptional gain they have managed to obtain.

And the win is not always about price accommodation but could be an additional service, a gift or another "extra mile" offer that the sales advisor has "up their sleeve" in order to close a sale.

- Feeling worth it

> *Lucy*: "Please let me introduce you to our Customer Care program. Not only will your leather creation bear an individual number, but we will be able to trace it and register it in our worldwide Customer Care system. Should you need to, you can have it repaired one day."
>
> *Lisa*: "Well, I hope I do not need to repair it!"
>
> *Lucy*: "You know, with time, there is always natural wear-and-tear and it's always good to know that we carefully crafted your bag and will take on this responsibility forever. Madame, welcome to our *Maison* and if you have any doubts or questions about your leather handbag, we organize, from time to time, visits to our expert saddlers and you will be invited to meet them and ask them any technical questions or even have your handbag examined."
>
> *Lisa*: "That's interesting."

Express at this closing phase the different extra services that come with the product. It allows customers to project themselves in time by explaining all the benefits they will enjoy after the purchase. There are always many possibilities to reward customers and which are not necessarily costly, as we will see in the next chapter - building loyalty.

5.7.3 Offer Financial Benefits

Facilitate Payment

Payment facilities are an easy and yet not commonly used facility available as a closing solution in the case of Luxury brands. In some countries, such as Japan and the USA, it's part of common retail practice. Payment facilities could be proposed with the cooperation of credit companies.

Proposing financing solutions is also an easy and effective way to close a sale.

> *Henry*: "Mr. Hudson we also extend our services to financing solutions. With your very exclusive choice we can offer you the best possible loan and insurance rate. You basically have different options depending on the initial down payment."
>
> *John*: "It's good to know. Are you offering a better rate than banks?"

Henry: "We are certainly offering very good rates. Nearly 100% of our customers choose to buy finance with us through our financial partners."

John: "Okay, that will be easier. Let me think about it and anyway it's not such an urgent decision to make."

Offer A Price Accommodation

Sometimes it is necessary to close with some price accommodation if it's expected and part of the company pricing strategy. Some important points to remember, as discussed extensively in the previous section, Step 5: Convincing, are to:

– Always give a reason for why you are granting a price accommodation
– Firmly limit your offer and do not open the door for further negotiation
– Secure a monetary deposit first

A deposit could be considered to be a financial benefit: customers can delay the payment to a certain date, but still secure a product. If the product is not available, the customer needs to pre-order and therefore a deposit is a must. In certain cases, customers won't want to make a full payment for the product in advance, being not yet 100% sure of the purchase decision. A deposit is a nice way to close a sale even if there is still some risk that the customer will change his mind and switch to another product.

5.7.4   Focus on the Decision Maker

As seen in the previous section, the real decision comes from a dynamic of three roles:

– The one who pays
– The one who decides
– The one who will own/use the product

And since customers might take the final decision as a couple, or even with friends, observing the group/family dynamic is key.

- Spouse Power

When a man shops with his wife, most of the time he is expecting agreement from his spouse or at least no disagreement. Never understate a woman's decision making power, even if the woman looks/seems/acts like she doesn't know about the product or will not be using it, or even paying for it. Believe it or not, she might be the one to make the final call.

- Friends and family test

When a customer arrives with friends and family, he most likely looks for reassurance or confirmation. Obviously, good service must be provided to all visitors. And it is necessary to describe all the benefits, and the reasons for the decision to purchase, to everyone in the friends and family entourage. They are here to help your customer to decide and most likely will state objections, to be certain that all aspects of the purchase have been covered. Deal with them softly and with diligence, as discussed in the previous section.

- The "dearest" is key

In the case of Mrs. and Mr. Taylor, if Michelle says "yes," it will be quite unlikely that Mr. Taylor will say "no." In the case of Mr. Hudson with his car purchase, if the children love the car, you can be quite certain that the parents will be more confident in taking their purchase decision.

5.7.5 To Win, You Need To Learn About Losing

Story Corner

The Emperor of the Kingdom Wu was at war against the Kingdom of the Chu. "What are our chances of winning?" Emperor Wu asked his Generals. "We are absolutely certain to win," answered all his Generals
The emperor asked the same question to his Prime Minister. The answer was the same.

"At the 1st battle, send only half the army and only the weakest of our soldiers", he ordered. Kingdom Wu lost the battle and the Generals were furious.

At the 2nd battle, the Emperor ordered his Generals to again send only half the army, and the oldest soldiers only. The Kingdom Wu lost another battle.

The Generals rebelled and all went to see Emperor Wu, to ask him to send the strongest of the soldiers. At the 3rd battle Emperor Wu ordered that they send all the soldiers, and that he would himself lead the soldiers in battle. The victory was magnificent: swift and more like a skirmish. The Kingdom of the Chu decided to surrender, having being totally demoralized by the 3rd battle, especially after two successful battles.

"Victory is not about a battle," Emperor Wu said, "but about a war. You need to know how to lose, in order to win."

- Explain the customer's gain – describe your loss

Henry: "John, I cannot give you more complimentary options than the fabulous four options I already managed to obtain for you from my Management."

John: "Come on, I am sure that your boss can make an extra effort."

Henry: "I made a calculation—the four options represent nearly 10% of the value of your automobile. It's a lot and really much higher than what we usually grant. A car showroom is a company with objectives and these options are not free for us, unfortunately. We have to purchase them and invest in you. As I mentioned, we consider it a necessary investment to gain the confidence of such valuable customers as you."

- Give an additional small gift

Lucy: "You know that I alone cannot offer you a 20% price accommodation. If I could, I would have done so already. We rarely mark down and have never yet on this iconic handbag."

Lisa: "Please ask your boss. I am a VIP in all the boutiques and I always get a special price."

Lucy: "Actually, I don't need to ask. Considering the fact that this is the first time you have visited us, and that you have shown a preference for our brand and in order to have you as part of our family, I can make an exception and grant you a VIP Privilege. Also, your choice today is particularly nice and we believe that having you choose our handbag is a plus for our brand. Exceptionally, and for this first handbag purchase, we can offer you a complimentary matching coin pouch."

Lisa: "That's it?"

Lucy: "It's a very nice gift and quite exceptional in our store. Thank you for choosing our brand. Here is an additional protective bag for you—it's also very nice. Are there any other items I can show you?"

Lisa: "Can I choose another color for the pouch?"

Lucy: "Yes, let's do it and I will take responsibility for it."

- Make a concession

Very often, by making the right concession at the end of the visit, the sales advisor is able to close the sale by making the customer happy. Concession is necessary and sales advisors need to have a number of possible concessions available for the final stages of the closing negotiations to finalize the sale. These concessions are the fruit of mutual benefits.

Henry:	"Mr. Hudson, we understand that you are a very busy and successful businessman and cannot spend much of your precious weekend checking on your car project. We want to thank you for signing today and I consulted my management for a special approval."
John:	"You mean that you have a gift for me?"
Henry:	"Yes, Mr. Hudson. We want to thank you for trusting us and to encourage you to take the decision right away with us, today. Is that okay with you?"
John:	"So what's my extra gift?"
Henry:	"We have already offered you four options that represented a 10% price accommodation, which is a lot as you know. We can also enroll you in our VIP Services Package, which will provide a great number of services."
John:	"It's offered to everyone, right?"
Henry:	"No, and it has a very important yearly value—it's part of one of the options we used to propose."
Henry:	"You did a great deal and thank you for your decision. We are all very pleased for you and truly believe you deserve it. Here is the contract and here are the key terms."
John:	"Looks like I have no choice now!"

- Grant rewards

Roger:	"Mr. Morgan, I have good news for you. Before your visit, I carefully reviewed your financial situation with us and made a report to my Management."
Paul:	"Very good! I have been with your bank for over 20 years"
Roger:	"Yes, Sir, and with impeccable records. We have decided to reward you with the lowest service charge possible which we reserve only for our very best and trusted clients."
Paul:	"Is this part of a selling trick or something?"
Roger:	"Definitely not. Even though you might find the reduction in charges is not big enough, keep in mind that it is still very significant especially you look at the long term, over a 15-year period."

Everyone likes rewards, especially when effort is recognized. For customers who are well known to you, think about how you can congratulate them—for what and how—so that it is meaningful for them. For new customers, you could reward them for their interest in your brand. You can also reward them in recognition of the quality of your clients (professional title, work profile, social status and so on). Or, simply reward them for taking the time to visit your brand: recognition is already a significant reward.

5.7.6 Key Words for Closing

The following is an example of closing in spite of hearing: "Let me think about it."

Allan Taylor:	"Let us think about it. We still have time, don't we darling?"
Michelle Taylor:	"Yes, it's so lovely but it's such an important decision!"
Alice:	"I understand that you don't want to regret your decision! If this should happen, I would also blame myself. I believe that we are the right brand for you and we did manage to find a piece that Michelle loves. With Mr. Taylor's invitation, I received exceptional approval from my Management for a special accommodation so as to welcome you to our brand. Your wedding anniversary is in a few days and this is a happy decision!"
Allan:	"Darling, what do you think?"
Michelle:	"Well, it's very nice for sure."
Alice:	"Let me book a nice restaurant for this evening for your celebration. Normally it has a 3-month waiting list. We have access for our best customers and you will see it's just the most exceptional place to be, when you are in Paris."
Allan Taylor:	"Well OK, let's do it."

5.8 Step 7: Building A Relationship

Customer relations is an important topic and we will cover the main aspects linked to Luxury Selling.

Unlike when selling fast-moving products, the sales advisor dealing with Luxury and high value products, has a rare chance to be able to have a real conversation with his customer and to take the necessary time to offer advice.

It's a genuine chance and a pleasure for the sales advisor who likes to interact. The opportunity to start to build a relationship is definitely the most rewarding aspect of a sales advisor's function.

5.8.1 Start A Relationship

We discussed in previous sections how to prepare oneself to inspire trust. We also insisted on the necessity of understanding an affluent customer's mindset in order to interact better. This relationship cannot be based on transactions only. It is also built on emotional resonance. An excellent sales advisor is able to inspire trust very quickly.

It is best to base the relationship on generosity—who refuses to be friends with someone who is generous, understanding and willing to help them? It's a heartfelt relationship, not simply one of client and customer. If a customer feels that the same sales advisor is someone nice, "with a good heart," the customer will feel safe, comfortable and offer their trust.

Faking sincerity is never good, and is a risky approach. Being candid, genuine and truthful are also rare qualities that you typically expect from a friend.

You can also try to find a "crossroad"—qualities that you both share. You may take notice of the different brands your customer wears—watches, bags, shoes—and if possible, and justifiable, start a conversation around your shared taste.

Observe your clients. There are certainly elements to notice and to compliment your customer on. By noticing these details you are showing interest and care. Complimenting your customer never hurts as long as the compliments are sincere and expressed appropriately.

Offering spontaneous assistance and services, by paying your customer attention in small doses from the beginning of the encounter, will reduce the brash commercial dimension.

Let's get back to Luxury selling situations.

> *Lucy*:   "It's a pleasure to have you today."
> *Lisa*:   "Thank you! I know—I gave you a hard time."
> *Lucy*:   "Not at all, I am really happy that I was able to assist you. I will contact you from time to time to give you good news, such as special event announcements or promotions."

Lisa:	"Yes, that would be nice."
Lucy:	"We also occasionally organize exclusive client events. Recently, we organized an Italian wine tasting with a female vintner and it was very enjoyable!"
Lisa:	"This sounds fantastic—in the store?"
Lucy:	"Yes! Lisa, what is the best way to contact you?"

To be able to start a relationship, you of course first need the agreement of your customer—which is translated by getting their contact information and approval for future contact. Obtaining these contact details is key and will very often determine the quality of the relationship.

- It's all about mobile communications. If possible, get three mobile communication contacts:

- Cell phone—ask for their cell phone number and reassure them that you will not call unless absolutely needed. Send a text message first.
- Social media platform—ask which is your customer's preferred platform.
- Email—ask for your customer's personal email address.

- It's about offering services

Provide reasons for asking for a customer's contact details. There are certainly many services to offer. Customers want to receive news of special promotions and events from you and pre-announce them.

- It's about being natural and friendly

The best way to get a customer's contact information is to remain natural and friendly when asking for it. There is no need for too many explanations or extra reassurance, when the relationship has already been established.

5.8.2 The Perfect Farewell

We have seen that at each step of Luxury selling, there is only one objective. The steps to achieving this are:

1. Preparation—To be ready
2. Welcoming—To deserve the customer's attention

3. Discovering—To know what to present to the customer
4. Presentation—To discover the customer's desires
5. Convincing—To reduce all possible fears
6. Closing—To get a buying decision or a genuine future consideration
7. Loyalty—To ensure customers return, soon or later

- When a customer has purchased

A purchase decision is a victory—not for the sales advisor but for the client! Customers experience immense pleasure during a visit and will enjoy the satisfaction brought about by acquiring the product for a long time to come. It's also an achievement: the customer had a need, a strong desire, and this was fulfilled perfectly.

The purchase decision is a success and should be congratulated, celebrated and rewarded.

- Congratulate sincerely

> *Martial*:   "Mr. Wang, I am Martial, and take care of this boutique. May I also introduce to you Patrick, who is our in store watchmaker. We are lucky to be able to have you visiting today. It's a great decision and we really want to warmly congratulate you."

The reasons to congratulate are various and it is always easy to find at least one:

- Right brand: "Congratulations, Lisa, and welcome to our brand. Your choice makes a very nice start because it really is the perfect brand for you."
- Right product: "Congratulations, Mr. Masson, for being able to find the right financial investment plan. It's not so easy and you made such an effort in achieving this important decision for yourself and also your family. "
- Right opportunity: "Congratulations Mr. Wang, for having a new brand to add to your very nice collection. Not many people are as discerning or make the right decision like you have."

- Celebrate warmly

> *Henry*:   "Mr. Hudson, we are so happy for you today. Let's celebrate this moment. I informed our Showroom Director, Sam, and he will join us right away."

John:	"Oh! no need. We are happy with our decision."
Sam:	"Mr. Hudson, I am Sam, and take care of this showroom. Congratulations! Alex and I are so lucky to have you and Mrs. Hudson here today. It's a great day. Actually, I want to offer you and Mrs. Hudson a nice dinner for two from a selection of restaurants that we believe are among the finest in town. We want you to celebrate and, again, thank you for coming to us."

A celebration is more than simply a congratulation—or nice words. A celebration is a happy moment, an instant that you do not forget. At this moment the Director and other sales advisors could gather to meet the clients and share a common celebration around a drink, a snack or a new service.

- Reward immediately

Lucy:	"Lisa, I have a surprise for you! As an Italian *Maison* we tried to identify the best Italian restaurant in town. We had shortlisted five of the best and we have an invitation for you to try one of them.
Lisa:	"This is so nice. Is it for two?"
Lucy:	"It's for one person for a lunch and the right opportunity for you to invite another person to discover the restaurant we recommend!"
Lisa:	"That's indeed a nice surprise, thank you!"

Company gifts are another creative thank you offer and will make the difference—customers always appreciate genuine gifts.
The reward could also be in the form of invitations.

Lucy:	"Another surprise Lisa is that we will have an in-store event next month and I would like to reserve a place for you if you agree. It's always very relaxed and an enjoyable quality moment."
Lucy:	"Okay, if I am in town, I will come and have a look."

This is also the perfect timing for invitations—future visit proposals. Customers tend to agree that they are flattered by the attention and special invites to attend future events. It's a rewarding gesture for the customer.

5.8.3 When A Customer Leaves Without Making A Purchase

When a customer has to leave without making a purchasing, in spite of the quality of the visit and the nice experience, it's never pleasant. And, it is somehow not an entirely successful experience; a truly happy one would be a purchase.

It's not a good moment for the sales advisor either. They may feel disappointed and perhaps slightly angry owing to a misunderstanding or a non-acceptance of the situation.

"Why did he/she not buy after that long presentation and explanation?"

"Why did he/she just walk away after showing so much interest?"

> ### Golden Rule
> Control your emotions when customers do not take a decision. Disappointment only leads to failure. Stay positive and keep focused.

It's therefore essential to get both parties back to a positive mood and mindset. In terms of the sales advisor's mood:

- Be grateful that the customer has already given their time and given you a chance to make a sale
- Be assured that nothing is ever lost, but will only create future opportunities
- Be nice. Don't ruin all your efforts when this is the beginning of a new relationship

- Thank the customer sincerely

In terms of farewell behavior, we advise you to remember to thank your customer warmly and sincerely. This may be expressed by generously offering your understanding and reassuring your customer of the value of the time spent together:

"I understand—it's such an important decision, that even if you love our product, you still need to take time to digest all this! It's a pleasure for me to have served you and I really thank you. I am sure that we will see each other again!"

The best way to show appreciation and gratitude is to offer help, even if the customer does not buy.

"It's raining outside—do you have an umbrella with you?"
"Would you like me to book a taxi for you?"

- Extend an offer

Any exceptional offer has a time limit! Prices can change and products can be sold. Therefore offer the customers the chance to reflect, but not for too long.

"Sir, the offer I just made you is, as mentioned, is exceptional and personal to you. It's normally valid only for today, as per the conversation with my Management. I can extend it, so as to have more time on your side, in order for you to be more familiar with the idea. Would two weeks be sufficient?"

- Book an appointment

To be sure that the visit and the momentum are not lost, you need to book another appointment with your client, or at least get approval for future contact. At this point in the visit, your customer is leaving and should willingly commit to come back.

Simply state why and how you will get in touch:

"I understand your time frame, Sir, and please allow me to give you a follow-up call in two weeks—just to know if there is anything I can help with. Thank you again for your interest."

Customers that leave without purchasing are sometime afraid that if they come back, they will have to buy. Therefore, make your invitation for their next visit non-committal and friendly.

"We will always be pleased to see you again! Do call in for a coffee, and please do feel free to bring along friends."

5.8.4 Keep A Relationship: Customer Relationship Management

The key to Customer Relationship Management is simply to have a relational plan. The relational plan is based on two primary components:

– Database (who and why)
– Relational plan (what and when)

5.8.5 Database

There is probably little need to explain why a customer database is important to a company. It is an essential tool for the sales advisor to fully succeed:

- Experience shows that even the best sales advisors can only manually—on paper—manage between 20 to 50 customers, which is typically insufficient.
- Having a well maintained database is a plus for the company but also for the sales advisor. It allows being able to refer to customer contact information with ease—and without the extra stress of having to remember all the client's details.

Each country has its own rules concerning privacy and personal information, therefore, we will only offer general guidelines and "golden rules" for succeeding in collecting database information and adhering to the typical opt-in rules.

Asking customers for personal information is sometimes seen as intrusive, but often this is more the perception of the sales advisor rather than the customer. It all depends on what the sales advisor intends to do with the customer's information and what offers the customer might receive. Customers do not want to miss any opportunities:

- Novelties
- Promotions
- Events
- Personalized information

From experience, and as a direct result of a positive customer experience, some trust has been established. If necessary, reassure the customer and leave the door open (Table 5.8.A):

Martial:	"Mr. Wang, I am Martial, and here are my contact details with my mobile number so please feel free to ring me for anything. May I also take your contact details because we would like to be able to provide you with all the services you deserve."
Peter:	"Okay. Here is my business card."
Martial:	"Thank you—may I also have your mobile number please?"
Peter:	"I am not used to giving out my mobile."

Table 5.8.A Customers' information

Type	Information Type	How to Obtain
Direct immediate contact	The most direct means are the most efficient: mobile, social media, email	Ask directly for the customer's cell phone number and preferred social media platform. Get an introduction from another sales advisor and extend your sales advisor social network
Indirect contact	Postal addresses are less important today. Contact Assistant and intermediate persons only if no other option is available	A home address is always sensitive information while not always being very useful. Avoid sending anything to a client's home address. Use only for very special occasions such as an invitation to an event
Quality of information	Customer purchase history, ethnic type, language preferences, age group, profession, residence country	Record all information from customers after conversations. A top sales advisor diligently notes all information obtained after each visit and records it in the database management system
Personal information	Private information such as taste/preferences, family members' names, anniversary dates and so on	Customers sometimes reveal a lot of private information. Research customers on the internet

Martial: "Mr. Wang, I will not call you unless absolutely necessary—only in the case of servicing or giving you exceptional offers that you won't want to miss."

Peter: "I receive so many spam calls, you cannot imagine."

Martial: "Be reassured, Mr. Wang. How can I keep on deserving your trust if I call you for just anything? Your mobile must be in Taiwan and starts with 852 right?"

5.8.6 Relational Plan

There is no real management of relations without a plan. A plan requires simply answering these questions in order:

— Who shall I contact?
— When shall I contact them during the coming 6–12 months?
— Which services should I offer?

The golden rules are as follows:

• Continuously contact all customers

Regardless of the frequency, a customer that you stop contacting becomes impossible to contact. Be sure to contact customers at least once every 6 months, as a general rule.

• Individually take care of your best customers

For your best customers you need to follow-up personally, with more frequent contact, such as once every 2–3 months.

• Adapt your frequency of contact to suit your top customers

Some customers need more frequent contact while others do not like to be disturbed. It involves a cautious analysis of all customers with a predetermined action plan by customer type.

• Share only good news

The quality of the contact, seen from the customer's point of view, is about what you bring to them each time. The good news could be a promotion, an invitation to an event, a free gift to pick-up and so forth.

• Be discreet

Never mention other customers, especially in front of a customer. Being absolutely discreet is not only an essential professional behavior; it is a virtue. Customers always avoid a too-talkative sales advisor. Discretion is 100% of the rule.

• Never insist, but never give up.

With affluent customers, patience is not only a must; it's one of the most important qualities of a talented sales advisor. Never continuously push an offer. But also, never give up on the relationship; keep on writing greeting cards even if you don't receive an answer. The effort will be in your favor.

Luxury selling is a real opportunity. The various encounters are enjoyable for those able to appreciate and realize them fully. It's not only about business but the possibility to meet new people—to build relations. That is also what gives meaning and content to life.

6

Conclusion

6.1 Happy Customers

Michelle and Allan Taylor are enjoying a beautiful dinner at a 3-star Michelin French restaurant. They dressed up for this special occasion. Michelle was splendid, with a dress she brought specially with her. It was perfect with her new necklace. Allan was merry. This was indeed an unforgettable evening. They sent a picture to their children in the USA. They also decided to send the picture of their happiness to Alice. Her advice had helped them to decide and she became part of the necklace story—their love story.

Lisa, after her trip to Moscow, decides to spend a few days in Lausanne, where she especially loves to stay at this charming palace hotel nearby the Lac Léman. She feels great with her new handbag. It is definitely the right color and she acknowledges to herself that "Lucy was right." It was a very good choice and she has already noticed that many women are looking at her alligator bag with envy. She has an appointment with Peter Wang to work on a new common project.

Lisa: "How was Geneva, Peter?"
Peter: "Some meetings with banks and investors, as usual."
Lisa: "Any new discoveries this time for your collection?"

© The Author(s) 2017   **209**
F. Srun, *Luxury Selling*, DOI 10.1007/978-3-319-45525-9_6

Peter: "Oh, yes, a new brand. Amazing! I had some doubt in the beginning but am now sure that this new watchmaking brand I found is worth collecting."

Lisa: "I am surprised that you are buying a new brand. You must have too much money burning a hole in your pocket!"

Peter: "I Know! The boutique manager, Martial, was amazing. He is so passionate. I couldn't resist and I am pretty surprised myself."

Lisa: "You mean impulse buying?"

Peter: "No, but I overcame my initial judgment and I now love it. A great experience!"

A Customer Who Buys Is A Happy Customer

Sophie and Thomas Williams are very happy about the house they are buying. It did involve a considerable budget change but, Simon, the real estate agent, was right. Not only do they need the large space to live in, but the house will certainly be a very good investment. On the day they need to sell it, they will call Simon. Besides, they have already introduced many colleagues and friends to Simon.

Happy customers become loyal and introduce more clients. It's a natural, virtuous circle of success. The more you sell, the more happy customers you have, and happy customers bring more customers, who then produce more sales.

6.2   Be Customer Focused

Successful sales advisors are customer focused. It also means that they manage to forget, for a while, about their immediate selling interest and are able to fully mobilize their intelligence to focus on their customers' motivations. Moreover, they focus on customers as people and not as clients.

They are able to detect desires, and to respond by tuning in to the customer's mindset. They manage to seduce naturally, combining charm and expertise. They are also able to understand their customers' fears—which are always deep-rooted. The capacity to reassure, is for a large part achieved with a warm "best possible friend" personality. The best sales advisors are spontaneous and generous, and even prove to be able to protect their customers.

See Customers Not Only As A Client But As A Person

6.3   Be Active In Selling

John Hudson joined his company's yearly sales convention in London, and Paul Morgan was there too. John had decided to invite Henry to speak to the company's sales team about his passion for selling cars. John loves the energy and also the elegance—the soft touch—of Henry's selling skills. John wanted Henry to inspire his company's sales force. Paul also believes that real success is created through teamwork between the Marketing and Sales Departments. He is very happy to see John proposing that Henry speak. He also believes that his industry should be inspired by different practices. At lunch, Paul mentions the great experience he had with his young private banker, who managed to enroll him in a 20-year savings plan. When Paul announced to his wife that he had subscribed to such a plan, his wife was touched by Paul's devotion to the family.

What are the common points among the best sales advisors? They have this incredible energy, combined with great professionalism. They are passionate about their brand and the products. They enjoy serving clients in the most meaningful sense of the word. They are also nice people who you can trust immediately. They know how to keep control, but never impose themselves.

Be Active In Selling: Be In Control Of Your Selling Success

6.4   Be Yourself

I want to end this book with an encouragement. The best sales advisors are naturally, simply, nice people. They are sophisticated and well presented, and speak well–elegantly and with simplicity. They are spontaneous, generous, and able to give before taking.

They are also able to understand customers' needs effortlessly because they genuinely care. They always influence respectfully and with a positive attitude. They also avoid possible conflict. Of course, they also know how to be the best partner in a decision when necessary, and always with long term vision for the relationship.

I believe that exercising the *métier* of sales advisor is not only complex, but also very meaningful. It's not only about selling techniques. It's also about being a good person and establishing good relations with other people. And, it is about managing to succeed with grace in every encounter.

Be A Nice Person With Natural Simplicity and Generosity.

Mark, you will remember, had enrolled himself in competing in marathons, with the first one in New York. He set himself an objective to run the most famous marathons around the world. It's a journey and the most difficult part is to start. The more marathons you run, the more you want to run. It's a positive addiction.

You took the decision about getting this book, and you read it. Congratulations on this achievement! Remember, the more you sell, the more you will know how to sell. Build momentum based on experimentation and exploration. Try new methods of selling and get into a process of constantly refining your selling style. There are many roads that lead to acquiring successful selling skills. You will find the most appropriate one for you in positively influencing customers and succeeding in every encounter.

Be An Active Learner: You Are The Actor Of Your Own Changes

I wish you every, and great success on your Luxury selling journey!

Index

© The Author(s) 2017
F. Srun, *Luxury Selling*, DOI 10.1007/978-3-319-45525-9

Printed by Printforce, the Netherlands